A LICENSE
TO STEAL

A License to Steal

Walter T. Shaw

with Mary Jane Robinson

Omega Publishing Group
303 Park Avenue South, Suite 1289
New York, New York, 10010

OMEGA PUBLISHING GROUP and
are registered trademarks of Omega Publishing Group (USA) Inc.

First Edition: March 2008

ISBN: 0-9786059-0-X
ISBN 13: 978-0-9-7860590-2

Jacket Design by Justin Bordeaux

Book Layout by Marion Webb Johnson

Library of Congress Control Number: 2007941522

Printed in the United States of America

10 9 8 7 6 5 4 3 2 1

For my parents, Betty Lou and Walter L. Shaw,
who would have appreciated the remarkable
journey it has been to try
to tell our story.

CONTENTS

PART THREE–REDEMPTION

FOREWORD

Redemption: To carry out; make good, fulfill

We redeem a promise by doing what we said we would do. This is what A *License to Steal* is all about. Full of love, fear, violence, hate and the quest for redemption, this book is an unbelievable journey through life.

Walter T. Shaw has been and is still on a journey that would fill ten men's lifetimes. From his early years as a boy growing up in a life full of turmoil, he watched his father, Walter L. Shaw, a true electronics genius, taken advantage of by the powers that be. Shaw Jr. was indelibly stamped with resentment and rage against them. This hatred turned the youngster into a man driven by vengeance to right the wrong that the world was doing to his father.

Though he worked tirelessly and legitimately to create his next breakthrough invention, Walter Sr. had the responsibility of a family to feed. He did whatever it took to keep them from going hungry, sometimes crossing over to the illegitimate side in desperation. In rebellion, Shaw Jr. decided to live his life on the wrong side after meeting some of the people who had hurt his father.

Most people are a little fearful of Walter Shaw because of his criminal background. Way down deep, though, he is a real, sincere person. Unfortunately, his honesty and sincerity are questioned because of his past, and he doesn't let too many people in. I met him around 1998 or 1999, through a mutual friend, and we talked about the movie he was producing based on this story. Walter asked me to play Anthony, a main character in the book, and I agreed because the script was so well written. A few years later, he invited me to come to Florida to pay tribute to his dad. Shaw Sr.'s thirty-nine patents were finally recognized, and Yaacov Heller's bust of him was unveiled that day. That's when I really became a friend of Walter's, realizing this journey he'd been on to redeem his relationship with his father.

This book will take you on the ride of your life. You will cry, you will laugh, and you will feel the love a family can have for one another, regardless of their circumstances. On a personal level, I can't wait to make the movie, *A License to Steal*. It's been a long time coming.

Frank Vincent
September 2007

"No one's life can be encompassed in one telling.
There is no way to give each year its allotted weight,
to include each event, each person
who helped to shape a lifetime.
What can be done is to be faithful in spirit
to the record, and try to find one's way
to the heart of the individual."

—Author Unknown

PART ONE

INJUSTICE

PREFACE TO PART ONE

"If I can draw it, I can make it."
Walter L. Shaw

My father had a favorite saying: "If I can draw it, I can make it." He always drew little sketches of his inventions first. "Thiel," he used to tell me, "if it works on paper, it'll work when I build it." And most of the time, it did. Even more amazing was the fact that he could think of it. As early as the 1940s, 1950s and 1960s, who was thinking of speakerphones, conference calls or call forwarding? My dad was ahead of the world by decades; his mind was going all the time.

It still hurts me to admit this, but as a kid I had no interest in what my father was doing. There was nothing in me that was curious about any of it. You know, "Show me what those two wires do," nothing. That stuff bored me. I was proud of his inventions, and I thought it was great that his mind could come up with those things, but "Show me how that works," never.

I remember sitting at the kitchen table when he was building his models and making plastic cases. He put his inventions in plastic cases to demonstrate how they worked, and just like his drawings, those cases were everywhere. They were glued together with model airplane glue, and the smell of that in the house was horrible. I can still see my dad sitting over there in his spaghetti strap T-shirts, just making those things. He sat there for hours and did that by himself. All hunched over with his hair flopping on his face, he would add the final touch and say, "Now it's ready to be demonstrated."

I did a cruel thing to my dad one time. It is fair to say that I did a lot of hurtful things to my father, but this one stands out. I always regretted it, still do, and I wish I'd told him that at the end.

My first wife, our new baby and I were staying with my mother and him in Findlay, Ohio, where Buckeye Communications was his newest backer. We were living in a tri-level house, and I heard my dad running downstairs in the middle of the night. He must have had a dream about what he was making at the time. The thing was built, but one piece was missing, and it came to him in his sleep. He's saying, "I got it! I got it! I got it!"

The next morning, he wakes me up all excited and says, "Thiel, I've got a demonstration for you!"

"Go ahead, Dad," I told him.

He called the weather, and he called the time. You used to be able to call a number for both of those, and he did it all on one line. He put one on hold while he dialed the other, and then he patched them in. That was his demonstration.

My father was so proud when he demonstrated the first conference call for me. Did you get that? My dad demonstrated the "first" conference call for me in 1967. I was there for that, but it was one of the few times I ever cussed around him. I said, "What? Are you kidding me? You woke me up for this? What the hell is that? Who cares about the weather and the time on one line?"

He said, "This is just a demonstration, Thiel, but if I can do it with the weather and the time, I can do it with other calls. More than two people can talk on one line with this little device."

"What's the big deal about that?" I asked him.

"You'll see," he told me, "this is going to be big."

That was it for me. I remember telling him, "Dad, I'm going home to Miami. It's twenty degrees outside, it's snowing up to your waist, and I hate this place. I'm packing up my wife and kid, and I'm going home."

"I'll follow you," he tells me, and we left at Christmastime.

Recognizing the commercial potential of his newest invention, the conference call, my dad broke with Buckeye

Communications to join two entrepreneurs. He would get screwed on that invention, too. The first was the speakerphone, which he invented in 1946, two years before my birth.

Chasing dollars. My dad was always chasing dollars that should have been his, and I was always running away with jewels that weren't mine. I had a favorite saying, too: "I live to steal, and I steal to live." That started for me in a big way when I made it back to Miami in 1967. After stealing tens of millions of dollars in jewelry with the "Dinnertime Burglars," it ended for me twenty-three years later.

United States Patent Office

3,389,224
Patented June 18, 1968

3,389,224
CONFERENCE CONNECTION AND CONTROL DE-
VICE FOR TELEPHONE SUBSCRIBER LINES
Walter H. Shaw, Miami, Fla., assignor to Shaw Electronics
Incorporated, a corporation of Florida
Filed Mar. 5, 1965, Ser. No. 437,443
4 Claims. (Cl. 179—1)

ABSTRACT OF THE DISCLOSURE

The invention consists of a conference connection and control device for telephone subscriber lines whereupon a controlling subscriber having a plurality of subscriber lines terminating at his set may interconnect these subscriber lines to form a conference circuit. The conference and control circuit consists of a pair of subscriber lines, that are terminated at the control subscribers set and under control of line button keys at the set, connected in parallel across the primary of a transformer and another pair of subscriber lines connected in parallel across the secondary. Each subscriber line is connected into the circuit and is under the control of a three position toggle switch. The switch has a "talk," "hold" and "disconnect" position. In the "hold" position, an indicator lamp approximately equal in impedance to a subscriber set is switched into the conference circuit. The control subscriber brings the other subscribers into the conference circuit individually and manually. The line button keys of the set connect the control subscriber to the various outgoing lines and the three position toggle switches hold the subscriber lines connected while the control subscriber is dialing out on another line.

My invention relates to telephone conference control circuitry and is directed particularly to a device for controlling conference connection with and among a plurality of remote telephone subscribers at a subscriber station having a plurality of telephone circuit subscriber lines.

The principal object of my invention is to provide a conference control device of the character above described that enables a subscriber at the controlling station to make successive outgoing cells to persons at a plurality of mutually remote stations to bring them into conference connection with him and with any or all of the other remote stations, selectively, and to selectively hold and disconnect each of the remote lines at will, whereby complete control of the telephone conference connection with respect to calling, holding, interconnecting for conference and disconnecting each of the individual remote stations called is maintained at the controlling station.

A more particular object is to provide a conference control device of the above nature which enables the controlling subscriber to place the plurality of calls to be brought into conference in the normal manner through local and/or toll lines of a telephone system over a like number of individual subscier lines at the controlling subscriber station, whereby each line can be controlled individually as to when it is brought into and dropped out of the conference connection for most economical use of toll line facilities of the telephone system.

Still another object is to provide a conference control device of the above nature wherein the status of each of the remote stations called into conference is controlled by an individual toggle switch having "talk," "hold" and "release" positions, each position of which is indicated or monitored by a single supervisory lamp, which lamp, in addition, serves as a terminal line impedance when its associated subscriber line is at "hold" position.

Yet another object is to provide a conference control device that is compact, simple to install and operate, and dependable and durable in use.

Other objects, features and advantages of the invention will be apparent from the following description when read with reference to the accompanying drawing, the single figure of which illustrates, schematically, the circuitry of a conference connection and control device embodying the invention.

Walter L. Shaw's first conference call patent,
filed March 5, 1965.

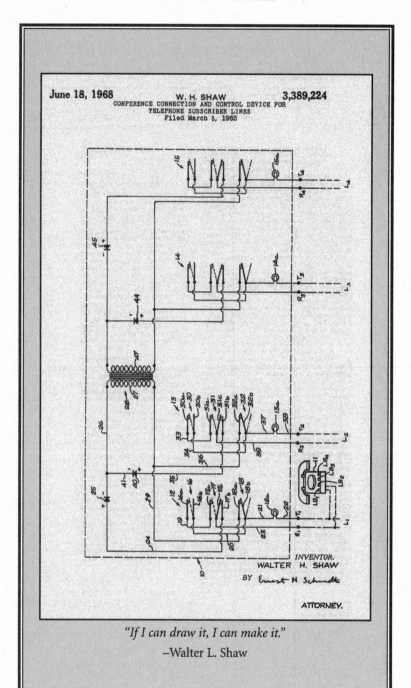

June 18, 1968   W. H. SHAW   3,389,224
CONFERENCE CONNECTION AND CONTROL DEVICE FOR
TELEPHONE SUBSCRIBER LINES
Filed March 5, 1965

INVENTOR.
WALTER H. SHAW
BY Ernest H Schmidt
ATTORNEY.

"If I can draw it, I can make it."
–Walter L. Shaw

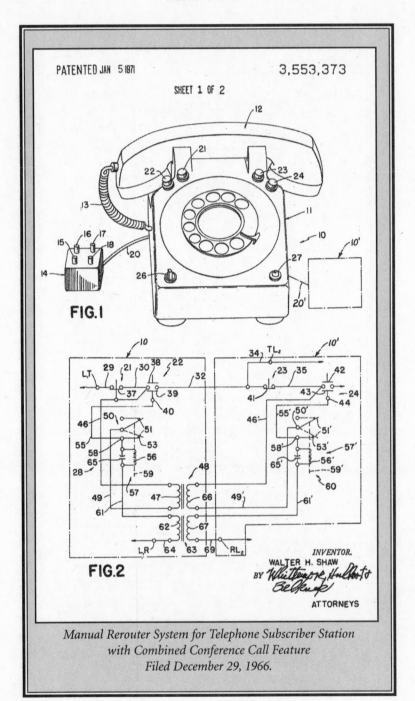

PATENTED JAN 5 1971   3,553,373

SHEET 1 OF 2

FIG.1

FIG.2

INVENTOR.
WALTER H. SHAW
BY *Whittemore, Hulbert &*
Belknap
ATTORNEYS

Manual Rerouter System for Telephone Subscriber Station
with Combined Conference Call Feature
Filed December 29, 1966.

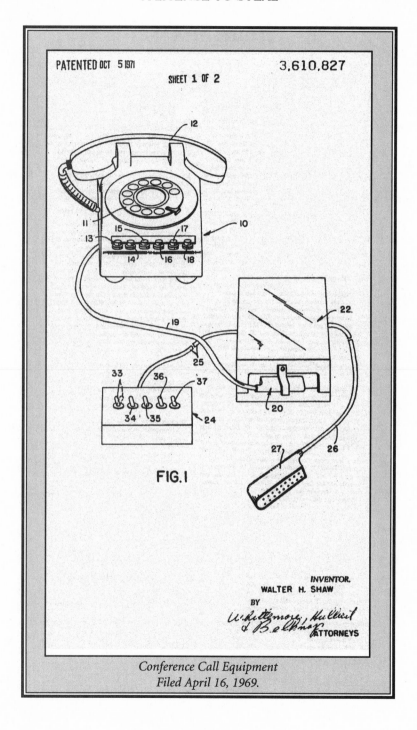

Conference Call Equipment
Filed April 16, 1969.

CHAPTER ONE

"They have a license to steal, but we don't need one."
—Carlo Gambino, Mafia Boss

A License to Steal, Walter T. Shaw's memoirs. Big deal. Who wants to read Walter T. Shaw's memoirs? Memoirs are all about remembering, and I don't like to go back. Why go through it again? I created a nightmare of a life for myself by doing some terrible things to people, and I justified my actions every time.

I still say it all started when I was a kid. It makes for a good story to tell about my week at the age of thirteen in the Old Senate Office Building in Washington, D.C. My dad was being questioned at the McClellan Subcommittee Hearings in August 1961, and I sat there looking at his back. The television cameras were turning, and they were asking him all kinds of questions about what he was doing with one of his inventions. I will never forget listening to all of that.

Named for Senator John L. McClellan because he chaired it, the McClellan Subcommittee opened Senate hearings on February 26, 1957, to investigate illegal activities in America's labor unions. When my dad was being questioned, though, the committee was looking into gambling and organized crime.

I will also never forget being out in the hall by myself one time, and the wise guys were all sitting in the atrium room waiting for their turn to testify. Carlo Gambino, Joseph Bonanno, and Archie Gianunzio were there. Known for being low-key, quiet and secretive, Gambino had recently become the boss of the Gambino crime family, and he was expanding his empire in the rackets in New York, Chicago, Los Angeles, Miami, Boston, San Francisco and Las Vegas. Gambling was one of Gambino's most profitable money-making operations. He wasn't there to testify, but he was concerned about the hearings.

In his thick Italian accent, Carlo stops me and says, "You remember one thing about these politicians, these judges, these big corporations. They have a license to steal, but we don't need one. You remember that. Your dad's not the bad guy, kid, they are. They're the bad guys."

Carlo Gambino was trying to cushion the blow for me; he saw me crying and upset about my father being beaten up like that. They were saying horrible things to him. I hated what the law represented. Of course, I also thought my dad was innocent, that he was just keeping his mouth shut because he hadn't done anything wrong. I didn't know he was protecting them. More on this later, but I didn't realize that Archie Gianunzio, a big-time bookmaker and my boyhood hero, had given him up. That wouldn't come out until years later, on what Archie called "truth day."

Anyway, on one of those days in D.C., general counsel Jerome S. Adlerman, asks my dad, "Did you make a device which could be attached to a telephone in such a way that it would not register as a toll charge but would show the busy signal, and you would be open to a line making a long distance call without the knowledge of the telephone company, without any toll charges or tax being paid to the Federal Government? I would like to warn you," he goes on to say, "This is an area where you might consider the advice of your counsel."

"I appreciate that. Thank you. This is where my counsel advised me I must refuse to answer on the grounds it might tend to incriminate me," says my dad.

Adlerman continues saying, "Very well. We have the proof here that you did invent such a device, and that this was the character of the device which has been used and has been seized in raids made by law enforcement officers. They found such a device,

My father testifying in August 1961.
(AP Images)

ASSOCIATED PRESS PHOTO   FROM WASHINGTON

INVENTOR TESTIFIES

Walter Shaw, Florida electronics inventor,
tells Senate Investigations Subcommittee,
at hearing in Washington August 28 that
he created a device used by some gamblers
to evade police wiretappers and cheat
telephone companies on long distance tolls.
He is awaiting trial in Florida on charges
growing out of use of the invention.

and the testimony before the committee is that you are the inventor of it."

"I have to follow counsel's advice on this," he tells them, invoking the Fifth again.

"Do you feel that it might tend to incriminate you if you answered truthfully the question: 'Are you the inventor of such a device?'" asks Adlerman.

"Yes, sir, I am the inventor," my dad admitted.

During the hearings, they usually called it the "black box" because that little apparatus was encased in a black Plexiglass case. Like I said, I didn't know it at the time, but my father had made the black box for the mob's bookmakers, for Archie Gianunzio, in particular.

At the end of the day, Senator McClellan says to him, "Some of the practices you have engaged in have led to trouble, don't you think?"

"Yes, sir," my dad agrees with him.

"You are kind of sorry about that, are you?" the chairman asks.

"One hundred percent," says my dad.

"One hundred percent sorry about it?" the senator repeats my dad's answer.

"Yes, sir."

Then McClellan says, "Try to go forth and sin no more."

What the hell was that supposed to mean? I was a kid; I thought my dad was innocent. Even though I learned differently, he will always be innocent in my mind. That black box was used for illegal purposes; that's a fact. And my dad had cracks, but he was never one of them, one of the wise guys; he was just trying to make ends meet for his family. Corporate America had screwed him early on, and it all started with Southern Bell Telephone and Telegraph Company.

Back in the 1940s, my father was working for Southern Bell, but he was always experimenting with electronics at home. In fact, he invented the speakerphone on his own time. Being the kind of guy he was, my dad naively demonstrated his invention to the powers that be at Bell. Within a day or two, he was presented with a new contract. They wanted him to sign away all his inventions— past, present and future. Rather than giving it all up to them, he walked, but they succeeded in blocking him from ever doing anything with the speakerphone.

I don't know if my father considered the devices he later made at the mob's request to be some kind of payback, but I can't believe he didn't feel that way. You know, *I'll show what my brains can really do.* I do know that he really suffered inside over the way Southern Bell mistreated him. It wasn't that he talked about it, but we could all feel it. I will always believe that Bell's treatment of him was the beginning of his undoing. Mine, too. He left them in 1950, and I turned to a life of crime seventeen years later. Unlike my dad, though, I was one of them, one of the wise guys.

People wanting to write things about me get all caught up in the whole mobster, jewel thief thing. Crime and brutality sells at the box office and the bookstores, but they miss the part about my dad and me. I can't deny that I was a criminal. I was deeply involved in the underworld, and I have been brutal, but this is a different story. This story is about two human beings. The people with a license to steal took everything from my dad. I didn't have a license to steal, and I wanted to take everything from the people who did. I wonder what my life would have been had corporate America not had its license to steal. I was too busy stealing without a license to figure that out.

When my dad was dying, one thing really stands out in my mind. He said, "Thiel, in the grand scheme of things it doesn't matter anymore. I hope you let all this go. I still have that 'Will Rogers mentality.'"

"What's that?" I asked him.

"Will Rogers said, 'I never met a man I didn't like,' and that's how I feel," he told me.

"You've been robbed all your life, and you still feel that way?"

"I still feel that way," he answered.

There was a time in my life that I really wanted to hurt people because of what they had done to my dad. I remember him telling me that he'd totally cut me off, even turn me in if I did anything like that. I would say, "You won't even defend us. You let people rob us, and you won't defend us."

"I can't think the way you think, son. It's not in my genes to think of hurting somebody," he told me.

Will Rogers had something else to say: "When you put down all the good things you ought to have done, and leave out the bad ones you did do—well, that's a memoir." He wrote that in his autobiography. I don't want this book to be written like that. My father did a lot of good things, but nobody gave him credit for them. Instead, everybody was always after him for the few mistakes he made. I want people to know all the good things he did. Walter L. Shaw had thirty-nine patents to his credit. He was an electronics genius. Like I said before, he was ahead of the world by decades, but nobody knows his name. That isn't right.

As for me, I know what I should have done with my life, and I didn't do any of it. Instead, I'm trying to make up for lost time. Keeping it real, though, I know I have to get into some of the bad stuff. In my time, I've been guilty of robbery, blackmail, extortion, forgery and counterfeiting, among other things. I've been a bad guy. No question.

When you pick up somebody's autobiography, even though they're telling the world what they want to tell and they're telling it like they want to tell it, you feel like you're getting in on something secret. It's like taking something you wouldn't have had otherwise, almost like having a license to steal. But life doesn't hand you only what you want it to hand you. Life doesn't keep secrets. It is what it is. I want to credit my dad with his due, and I want to exonerate him for having a son like me.

A wise guy said to me once, "Your love for your father goes deeper than a son's." He was right. I loved my father, but I probably admired him even more. In fact, I have always felt like his opposite. I knew he was all the things I was never going to be. Unlike what Will Rogers had to say about the subject, I'm not trying to write our memoirs, my dad's and mine; this is our story.

CHAPTER TWO

"All you have to do is have a guy that's full Italian make you:
your name's never going to get in your way."
—Anthony, Mafia Boss

My dad's mother, Mamie, came to America from Sicily as a young woman. She and my grandfather, Thiel Printzabella, ran off together. As my father told it, his parents had come across for a better life, the same reason they all came across. My grandfather was a poor peasant making sidewalks in Italy, and my grandmother was somebody's maid. They probably came in through Ellis Island in New York Harbor, so I've got the whole immigrant story behind me. Trying to make a new start over here, like so many of the immigrants did at the time, my grandfather changed his name. That's how we got the name Shaw.

When they arrived in America, my grandmother stayed home with their three kids, two daughters and a son. Born at home in Vineland, New Jersey, on December 20, 1917, my father had a hole in his heart, and they never thought he would survive. He was premature, too, only six or seven months along. Back then, there wasn't much hope for a premature baby. As tough as it sounds, my grandmother kept him warm in their oven, a makeshift incubator. His sisters helped take care of him, and they had to use women's handkerchiefs for diapers.

My dad was sickly as a kid, and from the very beginning, they hadn't given him a chance. That held true for the rest of his life. Not that he was sickly, that nobody gave him a chance. Except for the wise guys, nobody ever did give him a chance to make it, but that opportunity brought nothing but trouble to both of us. He worked so hard to come up with his inventions, but it was all for nothing.

As the story goes, my real grandfather took off when my dad was a teenager. Not too long after that, my nana (that's what I called my grandmother) married a plumber named Eddie Roberts, which meant she didn't have to go to work. I think he just provided some security for my grandmother. Eddie could feed three hungry kids, but he and my grandma slept in separate bedrooms. At fifteen or sixteen, a school dropout and working on the shore, my dad took off, too.

My father's full name was Walter Harvey Lewis Charles Shaw. I didn't know this until my nana told me, but she named my dad after all her brothers. In the Old Country, when an only daughter has brothers, she names her sons after all of them. His patents are registered in two different names. The National Inventors Hall of Fame in Akron, Ohio, called me about that. They said, "Your dad has some patents filed under Walter Lewis Shaw, and some under Walter Harvey Shaw."

"That's my father," I told them. They could tell it was the same person by looking at his birth date and Social Security number.

The National Inventors Hall of Fame is an organization that honors important inventors from all over the world. As of 2006, there have been 313 inductees. The only prerequisite of induction is being named an inventor on a U.S. patent, and the inductees are chosen by a national panel of inventors and scientists. The good thing is that posthumous induction is allowed, and I try every year to get my dad inducted in the annual ceremony. So far, I think it's his criminal record that's kept him out of the running—people always focus on the bad stuff—but I'll never stop trying.

Anyway, when I was thirteen, my dad and I were walking across the street in New York City, and I'll never forget it, he says, "You see that shriveled-up old man walking over there? That's your real grandfather." Nana told me that he showed up when I was born at Jackson Memorial Hospital in Miami on January 27,

1948. I was never clear on the story of how that happened, my dad and him being estranged like that, but his father saw me then. The only time I ever saw him, though, was from across the street in New York.

I remember being shocked the day we spotted him. I was just a little kid, and I wanted to run right over there, but my dad said, "I haven't spoken to my father since you were born. He ran away from us when I was a kid. Nobody's going over there."

The next year his sister called to say that they had found their dad frozen to death on the Bowery. Probably in his sixties by then, my grandfather was an alcoholic. Because he left the table, I didn't see it, but my dad must have broken down that day. I only saw that twice. The other time was when my mother died in 1986.

Except for telling me that his father joined the Rough Riders as a kid, my dad never talked about my grandfather. I don't know if that was true or not, him being a Rough Rider during the Spanish-American War, but that's all I ever knew about him. My father didn't want to cross that road for us to speak to him, but to his credit, he never said a bad thing about my grandfather. He even named me after him.

My parents named me Walter Thiel Shaw, after my father and my grandfather. My family calls me Thiel, but nobody else calls me that. My wife calls me Walter, but my first wife, my sisters and my aunt call me Thiel. Only one other person called me that, and that was Anthony, my boss.

My middle name was even used as a trick in case the FBI or the cops would come around pretending to be wise guys. If they said they had a message from Anthony, I would ask, "What name did he send you in?" They might say Walter or Archie, an alias I used, and I'd know it wasn't him. Anthony knew me only as Thiel. It was our little secret to know who was coming around, and that kept me out of trunks of cars.

I spent some time with Eddie Roberts, my father's stepfather. As a kid growing up, I really loved my grandmother, and I liked to hang around their house. It was a big deal to go visit them. It's funny what you remember. Nana had the bananas and the apples and the nuts and the nutcracker on her kitchen table. She had a washing machine, and she used an outside line to hang the clothes up to dry. Because she made her own pasta and bread, too, it seemed just like it must be in Italy. Her day started at five in the morning, and she was in bed by eight o'clock at night. My grandmother had a big influence on me.

My mother, though, tried to keep me away from their house. She didn't like me being with them, and my mom could be harsh at times. My mom liked her mother-in-law as a person, but she was ashamed of her lack of education and ignorance about some things. In fact, when she was mad at my dad my mother called him "illiterate." She was really talking about his family, and he knew that.

My mom had a bit of a temper, and she could lash out and chop you up with her words. She didn't mean any harm though. She was quick to rile, but she was also quick to forgive. That was her good side. She would forgive you in a minute if you apologized, or if she thought she was wrong. I really loved my mother.

I'll admit to seeing some of what she was saying about my dad's family when I was a kid. My grandmother would say to my dad, "Hey, Wally-o, when you gonna come and see your mama?" That's the way she talked. She called him Wally-o, the Italian form of Walter. My mother never liked that.

My grandmother spoke with that broken English, too, to the day she died, and it annoyed the hell out of me. The Italian was long gone. My dad understood some Italian, but he didn't speak it. "If you come to America, you do what Americans do, and you learn English," my mother used to say. His whole life, though, my father regretted that he never learned his language, but neither he nor I ever went to Sicily.

It was actually hard to believe that my dad came from those beginnings, living with immigrants and all that. He was very polished, every bit a gentleman. My dad was a class act all the way. His lawyer represented him for fifty-two years, and he wrote a beautiful letter to me a few years after my father died. He said, "I can never remember Walter Shaw without a broad, warm smile and a cordial handshake. To say the least, life was not kind to him. Even while terminally ill, though, he suffered in silence."

I really don't know where he got that, but he was always that way. It just seemed that there was something natural in my father to act sophisticated and gentlemanly. He opened doors for the ladies, and he always dressed in suits. My dad knew what to do when it came to manners. Even at the McClellan Hearings he kept saying to all of them, "Thank you, sir." He didn't get that from his mother, but that never stopped me from wanting to be with her.

When he went to prison the first time, I ended up moving into my grandmother's place. Ironically, my dad had left her home when he was sixteen, and I went to live with her at the same age. She was dying of cancer, and I took care of her while I was there. My grandfather died of cancer, too. I've got a thing for the elderly. Who's going to take care of them? We throw them away like used goods. I definitely have a soft spot for old people.

This is getting off the subject, but I remember casing an old lady's house in Fort Lauderdale. My guys and I went to a thirty-five-acre estate on the Lauderdale "strip," doing our homework before we did the place. It was the first big estate built on the water, in 1919, or something like that. Because it was deeded to the Florida Trust for Historic Preservation, the property was open to the public for tours, but the old heiress still lived there in private quarters. We went on one of those tours, and I remember seeing her there. I couldn't rob a ninety-year-old lady, so I called my crew off the job.

Nathaniel L. Barone, Jr.
ATTORNEY AT LAW

250 BIRD ROAD, SUITE 302
Coral Gables, Florida 33146

TEL: (305) 443-9868
FAX: (305) 443-5665

August 30, 1999

Walter Shaw, Jr.

Dear Walter:

Walter Shaw was a man out of step with the times in which he lived. I say that because in the world of electronics he was far ahead of the rest of scientific community. The concepts we have today of voice and data transmission, which we accept as common place, were his some 25 years ago. Unfortunately, as is true of many geniuses, the world was not ready to acknowledge it.

Walter was unique, not only in that he was talented, but he was a good human being. His children, friends and those who knew him will remember him as a kind, loving, man who saw the best in everyone. Always giving of himself, his nature was unselfish and generous to a fault. If he was hurt or was suffering he did it in silence. I am sure that the fact that both he and his wife were both religious was reflected in his personality.

I am sorry to say, and it hurts me deeply, that these same qualities which most of us respected and admired made him vulnerable to those among us who considered it as an opportunity to exploit. Regardless of what life dealt him, whether it be personal, in the scientific community or in business, I can never remember Walter Shaw without a broad, warm smile and a cordial handshake. To say the least, life was not kind to him. Even while terminally ill he suffered in silence.

Walter Shaw, to me was a friend, someone who will be missed and who I must say will always be remembered. My most fervent hope is that in some small way that anything that is said or written about Walter will show him for what he was, someone who opened a door to the electronic age, a pioneer.

Sincerely yours,

Nathaniel L. Barone, Jr.

NLB/mda

A letter from my father's attorney of fifty-two years.

Anyway, like I said, my dad worked on the Jersey shore when he left home. He was robust and athletic. He always ran on the beach, and he loved doing his calisthenics. I remember him saying, "I worked hard on the fishing piers as a kid. You take care of your body when you are young, Thiel, and the body will take care of you when you're old." He had all kinds of clichés. The only time I was taking care of my body by running on the beach, I was training for a very different reason. I had to be able to run fast to flee the scene of a crime. It's not easy to admit this, but in all honesty, I quit my career as a cat burglar because I couldn't run fast enough anymore.

Going back to my name, when I saw the road I was going down, I was worried I'd never get made because my last name was Shaw. Getting made means you have taken the oath in the underworld. Even though John Gotti was Jewish and Italian, he later became boss of the Gambino crime family, but I was concerned about my name. My father and grandfather were full-blooded Sicilian, but I've gone through life with the name of a Scotsman. I always had to explain the name "Shaw" to my associates.

In later years, I questioned my boss, Anthony (whose last name is omitted out of respect) about that, and he says, "Listen, there's rules for everything, but we make exceptions when you really got the heart. All you have to do is have a guy that's full Italian claim you and make you. Your name's never going to get in your way. If I want to make you, I can. I'm not saying I am making you, but I'm saying that's the way it works." So the name didn't matter.

CHAPTER THREE

"This is a family that loves each other,
and that's all you need in life."
—Betty Lou Shaw

In her youth, my mother, Betty Lou Roberts, was a dead ringer for Olivia de Havilland. It was just a coincidence that she had the same last name as my nana's second husband, my father's step-father, Eddie Roberts. My mom was Bahamian and English, and her parents, Jenny and Birge Roberts, were born on Turtle Key Island in the Bahamas. My grandfather's brother was very wealthy, and he was over in Miami, Florida, so my grandfather came over, too.

My mom and her only sister were born in Miami, where Grandpa Roberts was a barber first, and then he became a Singer Sewing Machine representative. For some reason, even though Birge was their father's first name, the kids in the neighborhood called my mother and her sister the "Birge" sisters. I never understood that.

My dad had been an engineer for Southern Bell in Key West, and he helped design the cable that goes underneath the ocean to the Bell housing on this side. He had been married before he met my mother, and when he came home from Key West unexpectedly, he found his wife in bed with another guy. Naturally, to my dad's way of thinking, that was immediate grounds for divorce.

Before all that happened, though, he lived next door to my mother and her parents. That was on Flagler Street in Miami. My dad asked this kid, the paperboy, "What's that girl's name?"

He says, "Betty Lou Roberts."

"How old is she?" my dad asks him.

"Thirteen," he says.

"She's mature for her age." My dad was nineteen then, but he didn't forget the name Betty Lou. Turns out, she didn't forget his name, either.

So my dad meets my mother briefly in 1936. Before they got together, though, she would go off and get married, and he would go off and get married. I have a half-sister from my dad's first marriage, Susan, but my dad never claimed her because his wife slept around. Even so, my nana always wanted me to know Susan. I met her twice, but she was a lot older than me. Her mother's name was Pam, and she always brought her over to my grandmother's house. My dad would never be there when that happened. Susan called him Dad, but he never accepted her as his kid. Funny thing is, she looked like my father. One time I said to him, "She looks like you, Dad." He saw that, too, but he didn't want anything to do with that marriage because of the adultery.

Anyway, my mother had married Lamont Haas, a dentist fresh out of dental school, and they had my older half-sister, Linda. When World War II started, even though she begged him not to, my mother's husband joined the service. Because he was a dentist, he was made an officer, a lieutenant, and he became a pilot in Germany. His brother was a missionary, a Christian, born again. Grandpa Roberts was a Christian man. My grandmother and him were both big-time, huge Christians. They were Plymouth Brethren. No music was allowed in their faith. And my mother was always at church. In fact, that's where she met Lamont Haas.

My mom's parents were very moral people. Staunch in their beliefs, they were also very stern. They wanted us to be better people than those who didn't know about being moral, Christian people. I admired them for that, but they obviously had no influence over me in my early life.

So Lamont Haas was well-educated, but my mother had only graduated from high school. They fell madly in love anyway, then he goes off to war, and my mother is heartbroken. She begged him, saying, "Please don't go. Why are you doing this?"

"The country needs me," he told her. I heard this story a lot as a kid.

On his last mission before coming home he was the captain of the plane, and they were flying in formation. He trades places with another pilot, that one falls asleep, the wing of the next plane hits Lamont's side, and he was killed instantly. Lamont was the only one killed on the plane.

My mother said she knew he was dead the minute the military car drove up to the house. She saw the car coming up the driveway. The brass got that kind of treatment. They came to the door instead of sending a telegram to tell the family about the death of their loved one.

Needless to say, out of earshot my mother told me that story many times. "You know why I lost him?" she would ask me. "Because he was too good for me," she says. "That's why I lost him. God took him home because of my hurtful tongue. That's why he took him from me." Like I said, my mother could be harsh at times.

I think Linda always thought she got shortchanged. She was only two when he died so she never knew her real father, but she made sure she knew her uncle and her paternal grandparents. Linda spent time with them sometimes. His only child, she looked just like her father. I saw the wedding pictures, and he was wearing his uniform. Blond wavy hair, both of them had that. He was definitely a handsome man. She got the personality of that family, too.

As the story goes, years later my dad's divorced, my mother's a young widow, and he spots her sitting in a drugstore one day. He looks over, and he asks her, "Aren't you little Betty Lou?"

She says, "Yes, I am. Walter?"

"Yeah," he says. By then my mom was in her twenties, and my dad was probably thirty or so. They started seeing each other, and one thing led to another.

The whole time my mom and dad were courting her parents wouldn't speak to him. My mother's parents were good people, but they never approved of my father. He was Italian, and they didn't like that. They called him a greasy Italian and said she shouldn't be marrying a foreigner. They'd even cross over to the other side of the street to avoid him. I resented that. That would be the rub all my life. I always had to hear all the negative stories about my dad, all the things he did wrong. That started with seeing how my maternal grandparents mistreated him. I can imagine how hurtful that must have been for him. He was just trying to make it, you know, and my mother loved him.

My mother was a romantic. She was a real movie buff, and she couldn't get enough of the love stories. She identified with love stories, and unbelievably, she made like she had a fairy tale life. "God blessed me with two wonderful men. I love your father as much as I loved Monty, just in a different way." I remember her saying that to me all the time. "Your dad is a rugged man's man, and Monty was handsome. God sent me the perfect man to make up for Monty." That's just how she was. She saw what my father was made of, and she fell in love with his insides.

I remember my mother saying to me so many times, "Thiel, we may not have all the material things, but you know what you come from? This is a family that loves each other, and that's all you need in life. You don't need anything else." That wasn't true for me. I needed something else, and I regret that my mother had to live with that fact.

Betty Lou and Walter L. Shaw with Vonn, the boxer.
"My parents really loved each other."

CHAPTER FOUR

"You did this on your off-time?"
—Executive, Southern Bell Telephone and Telegraph Company

My father was planning to go into the service when he left home at the age of sixteen, which would have been before World War II, but he had a hip that was off. Back in those days, you had to be 100 percent physically fit to join the military. That's why he ended up going to work on the shore. After doing that for a while, he started to work for Western Electric as a stringer. Stringing cable and lines, he made a penny a mile. My dad was fascinated with electronics.

During the Great Depression, he used to go to a movie for a nickel. I remember him saying to me, "A nickel was a big deal back then. Those were hard times to live through." Fortunately for him, he managed to keep his Western Electric job during the worst of the Depression years, the early 1930s.

Then one day in 1936, he spoke to a telephone lineman on the street. The guy was climbing poles, and my dad asked, "What do I have to do to do that?"

The guy said to him, "You're already working for Western Electric as a stringer. Get a hold of Southern Bell and see if you can get into their system. You may get a job working with them."

When he was just twenty-one, my dad landed a job with Southern Bell in Miami, and that's how it all started. He got into their system all right, in ways that would hurt him for the rest of his life. Bell was just the beginning of his troubles.

Walter Gifford, the president of American Telephone and Telegraph Company, established Bell Telephone Laboratories in 1925. It would take over all the work being done by the engineering department's research division at Western Electric. That meant that the ownership of Bell Labs was split evenly between AT&T and Western Electric. Its principal work was to design and support the equipment Western Electric built for Bell System operating companies.

Southern Bell Telephone & Telegraph Company was the Bell operating company serving most of the South at that time. They provided telephone service to Georgia, Alabama, Florida, North Carolina, South Carolina, Kentucky, Mississippi, Tennessee and Louisiana. Remember, my dad wasn't educated. He quit school when he left home, so he started going to Bell Laboratories Night School in Miami.

My father made excellent grades at Bell Labs. In fact, he earned his high school equivalent degree, too, which is another thing we had in common, and when he graduated he had four years of calculus under his belt. That's how smart he was in math. People always said he was a genius.

It wasn't long before they took him out of the field as an installer and a lineman, and they put him in Bell Labs as an equipment engineer. At its peak, Bell Labs was the top facility of its type, and all kinds of revolutionary technologies were being developed. They saw his potential and were quick to put him there, but he had no idea what it would cost him.

My dad was fourteen years with Bell Labs, and on his off time he was experimenting. He would buy relays, capacitors, and transistors—all kinds of parts that could make things. One of the first things he made, which I mentioned earlier, was the prototype of a speakerphone. Nobody knows that Walter L. Shaw made the very first hands-free speakerphone. You didn't know that, did you? It was the first of its kind.

That's another thing that came up at the McClellan Hearings. The general counsel, Jerome Adlerman, asks him, "Have you obtained any patents for telephonic devices?"

"Yes, sir," my dad says.

"And one of the devices is an automatic speaking arrangement?" asks Adlerman.

"That is correct."

Mr. Adlerman goes on asking him, "You can have the telephone on the desk and in other areas of the room, and without lifting the receiver you can talk over the telephone and listen to conversations?"

"That is correct," says my father.

"When did you invent that Mr. Shaw?"

"I started on that in 1946, and I filed for patents in 1947," he tells them.

When my father took that invention into the senior guys at Southern Bell, they were frightened by it. The head guy asked him, "You did this on your off-time?"

He says, "Yes, sir, I did."

"Well, young Walter, (that's what one of the senior engineers called him), great presentation. Get back to us in a couple of days on this."

He got back to them in a couple of days, and that's when they had that contract I mentioned waiting for him. Now, he's already married to my mother, and I'd been born in 1948. This went down in 1950, so my dad was thirty-three by then. As the story goes, the contract they wanted him to sign would give Bell the rights to all past, present, and future developments he made on their time— *and his time.* That would include the speakerphone he had just demonstrated to them, and my dad wanted to think about it. So he goes home and talks to my mother, and years later they were still arguing about that.

My dad had a good-paying job, and when he married my mother he had $27,000 saved, which was a lot of money at that time. They had bought their first house for eleven grand—cash.

My father had a very easygoing personality, and everybody liked him. He was kind, mild mannered, the Gary Cooper type, but he says, "I'm not going to do it. I'm not going to sign their contract. I'm going to go off on my own."

When he checked back with the executives at Southern Bell, they told him, "Don't try to hook that thing up. We'll never approve of that being hooked up to our lines."

"Well, we'll see about that," he answered them, and he was on his own in 1950. He lost his guaranteed income, and my father ventured out into the communications market as an independent. That was the beginning of his journey, and my parents argued a lot about that not being a wise decision. It may be surprising that it was my mother who actually got him to leave Southern Bell. He was the one blaming her when they argued about it. They were just words, but I remember that. My mother was proud to death of my dad; she was behind him 150 percent. In fact, she addressed all her letters to him, "Your darling wife to her inventive husband."

After leaving Bell, my dad worked hard to get his speaker-phone off the ground. Even Senator McClellan asked him about that at the hearings. He said, "Were you able to sell that, to market it to the telephone company or to any manufacturing producer?"

My dad said, "Well, after several years of perfecting it, I had many consultations with other inventors of various telephonic equipment, and they suggested that the best procedure to follow would be to try to set up your own company and get into actual development and production of it, and then create a sales organization to supply independent telephone company users as well as industrial telephone users of various types of equipment."

"So it was to use it primarily for a legitimate purpose to begin with?" asked McClellan.

"To begin with, and 100 percent all the time," my dad told him.

"To begin with, 100 hundred percent," said McClellan.

And my dad finished his sentence, saying, "All the time."

As a matter of fact, he did try to set up a company called Shaw-Tel to manufacture the speakerphone, but Bell stopped him every time he got close. A lot of men lost money on that deal.

I think all of his inventions meant something to him, but I know he was really proud of that one. I can't document this, but my father told me the story behind the speakerphone. A guy who owned a pro football team had a wife with polio. There was no vaccine for polio until Jonas Salk came up with it in 1952. Some polio victims were living in iron lungs. This guy's wife was one of them, and he came to my dad and asked him, "Can you make something that my wife can use to talk to her children on the phone? She can't even use the phone."

I love the significance of that story. My dad originally invented the speakerphone for people who were living in iron lungs, strapped to a machine. It was voice activated, and he called it the voice automatic loud-speaking telephone. It was finally patented on November 20, 1951, Patent No. 2,575,844, and he called it the Feedback Neutralization Means for Telephone Systems.

When his hopes for financial rewards from the speakerphone collapsed, my father opened up a TV store, one of the first Philco television stores in Miami. He did all kinds of things just trying to make it. I mean, he was involved in anything to do with electronics. One time he even bought an old electronics warehouse that was going out of business. My dad was never going to come out of that field, but all he ever really wanted to do was invent things. He wasn't making it as a small businessman. Never would make it as a businessman of any kind.

So there was the speakerphone, and he also did something for a major toy manufacturer early on. It was a helmet with a visor, and there were things inside for kids to talk to each other. It was the very first headset where you could communicate without an antenna. He filed for that patent on December 14, 1953, and it was issued on July 22, 1958. That one was called the Two-Way Communication Unit, Patent No. 2,844,659, but he never saw the financial reward for that one, either.

As a kid, I met some of the patent attorneys he consulted. I remember listening to their nonsense. They would say to him, "You've got to be more of a businessman than an inventor, Walter. They are going to beat you up, take you and rob you blind." I grew up with that.

My dad's gentle demeanor and laid back attitude used to infuriate my mother. She was always arguing with him about his being too naïve. He was so gullible. He'd believe that they made Swiss cheese out of the moon. My father always took people at face value and agreed on deals with a handshake. "You're so trusting. A handshake means nothing!" my mom would tell him. It drove her nuts, but she loved him anyway.

Even the patent attorney, David A. Gast, in the statement he prepared for my father's nomination for induction into the National Inventors Hall of Fame, said, "Sadly, the barrier built by Mr. Shaw's humble nature prohibited him and his inventions from receiving, during his lifetime, the recognition that he was so deserving of." That's just the way he was. He trusted everyone and expected to be treated fairly.

It was definitely my mother who taught me never to trust anyone. "If you don't trust them, they can't hurt you, Thiel." I learned from her not to get too close to anybody. "They'll know your dirt and tell people. If you don't want your thoughts told, don't get close to anybody." So I didn't. I always covered myself. They could come within a certain perimeter, and that was it. Even my wife, she's as far as she can go. She'd tell you that, too.

My mom was very shrewd, and she could read people at twenty yards. Her intuitions were rarely wrong. Sometimes she'd miss it, but that was one out of a thousand. She would tell my dad,

"I don't trust this guy. He's gonna bite you." She saw things coming before he did, but I never heard her rubbing that in to him.

I got my intuition from my mother. I have always been able to read people, and that's another thing that kept me out of trunks of cars through the years. I could read a guy before he could read me. That was the only way to survive in my business.

I think my dad always thought he might have done better if he had stayed on as a company man with Southern Bell. Personally, I don't think my dad would have been a good company man, not in those times. He wasn't that kind of guy. The problem was that, just like different attorneys told him, he wasn't a good businessman, either. My dad was a scientist, an inventor. Walter L. Shaw was a genius inventor. That's what he was. He was always testing something. He would stay up all night testing something. That was his joy.

My primary memory of my father has him demonstrating things. He had a laboratory every place we lived. His inventions were his life. I also remember that he was always going to the airport chasing money down somewhere for financing. He was constantly looking for backers to finance his ventures. We were always going someplace when I was a kid. There was nothing stable about my childhood—nothing. Always looking for that pot of gold, he wanted to better our situation, to make us financially secure.

I get what his frustration must have been like. I've been chasing dollars for the last nineteen years trying to finance a movie about him and me, and I'll get to that later. With my past being what it is, though, it's been hell trying to get somebody to believe in me. They believe in the story, but they don't believe in me. My dad's past is held against him, too, but he always saw the glass as half full. Never saw it any other way.

Like he told me, "I never met a man I didn't like. I still have that 'Will Rogers mentality,'" he said to me on his deathbed. He was a different guy that way.

My father's childhood was impoverished. They were poor immigrants, and he didn't want us to live that way. He wanted his life in America to be the American dream. My dad was always chasing the dream. He found only one way to prosperity, though, and it wasn't a rainbow that led him to that pot of gold. It was the Mafia, but the prosperity didn't last long. What lasted a lifetime was the stigma from his association with organized crime.

Had my dad been a company man or a businessman, I know that our story would have been different. Because of the way he was treated, all of his genius inventions did nothing for us, and my childhood was impoverished, too. If there is any excuse for the miserable things I've done, it was sparing my kids from knowing the childhood I knew. At any cost, stealing was all about what it would do for my family, how we were going to live, and have the lifestyle that was not available to me as a kid.

I'm at the end of my life, and the majority of my time on this earth has been wasted. I know my life could have been different, but that doesn't matter. I'm just hoping that telling this story might make my father's legacy something different. Just like his dad, my father was destitute when he died in 1996, and I'm still fighting to get him recognized. He patented thirty-nine inventions, but on his last flight home to Florida he got off the plane with holes in his shoes.

My father and me at the Jersey Shore in 1952.

CHAPTER FIVE

"I'm strong to da finich, 'cause I eats me Wheatina."
—Popeye

U ntil I reached the age of two or three, my dad was still working for Bell. He didn't leave them until 1950, and naturally,
I don't recall much about those years. When I try to come up with
early memories of being with my father, I can remember when he
carried me on his shoulders into the ocean on the Jersey Shore. I
was a kid, still innocent. That is probably my only memory of
being really innocent.

We stayed in Miami for a couple of years after he quit his job.
My dad never made it with the speakerphone, and his TV store
went bust, so he was available when the government called on him
in the early 1950s. After World War II, there was a lot of military
construction going on in this country. Many of the radar stations
in Alaska became operational in 1952-1953. Alaska was still sover-
eign ground then, Indian land. It didn't become a state until
January 3, 1959.

It was great to have radar as an early warning system, but we
also needed a communications system to keep us on alert. My dad
was involved in that, and he was asked to go to Elmendorf Air
Base, a big Air Force installation in Alaska, to work on what was
called the White Alice Communications System (WACS).

Somebody had heard about my father's earlier employment
with Southern Bell, and they said he was one of the brightest engineers to come out of Bell Labs. If anybody knew how to get the
glitch out of the system, this guy would be the one. They saw
potential in him. So it goes that my dad was asked to go to Alaska
to work on that with the United States Air Force. There were lots

of brainy engineers working up there; he was one of them, and one of the youngest.

The majority of the radar installation locations up there were a great distance from the nearest telephone land lines. Because of that, construction on the tropospheric scatter system, which is what they called it, began in the summer of 1954, but we were there before that. That system could scatter distant television and radio stations by the troposphere, which meant they could travel farther than the line of sight. Large tropospheric scatter antennas could connect remote Air Force installations in Alaska, and they could also be used for civilian phone calls across the entire northern portion of North America.

In the 1950s, Alaska had only basic telephone communication systems. As a matter of fact, until the tropospheric scatter system was developed, only one phone call at a time could be placed from Fairbanks to Nome. So you can see why my dad was interested in that project up there.

The American government can do anything it wants to do, and President Dwight D. Eisenhower put my father in a certain class so he could live on the base with his family. He was even given the rank of colonel, but he didn't get any military benefits or anything like that. All he got was his title.

My dad wasn't going to go in as an underling, wasn't going to be just an employee. That was part of the condition of his accepting the work. He says, "You know, if you want me to go, I'll gladly go for the country, but I'm going to go where I'm the supervisor in charge. I know how to make this thing work." So they agreed to make him Colonel Walter L. Shaw, a chief engineer on the alert system, and that gave him some respect.

My mom, Linda, and I went with him to Alaska, until the earthquakes scared my mother out of there. She didn't want to go there in the first place; she knew about the earthquakes. We went anyway, and I vaguely remember them bringing us in by a B-52. We were staying on the base in what seemed like a hotel. After we got there, we had the first earthquake, and it shook my mother, so to speak. Then the second one rattled her big time. A third one came right behind it, and she said, "I'm leaving." I was probably five or six by then. I can't say I remember the earthquakes, but I remember hearing about them.

My health problems had something to do with our leaving, too. I started getting sick with earaches and strep throat on Elmendorf Air Force Base, and that always plagued me as a kid. When we left, my dad stayed on to finish the job. He didn't pull out with my mom, my sister and me.

I don't really remember anything about my childhood before my father was doing the Eisenhower project. That ended about the time I started school, and I do remember my early school years. Until I was eleven, we were moving around a lot. I don't think it's a stretch to say that I was in eleven different first grades. Every time my dad had a potential investor, we moved to that city. My aunt called us a bunch of gypsies. More than the others, I remember East Orange and Newark in New Jersey. My younger sister, Crystal, was born when we were living in East Orange, in 1957, when my mother was thirty-six or thirty-seven. To my knowledge, she wasn't planned. After that we moved to Newark, where my dad tried to make it with a surplus TV store. Eventually, we moved back to Florida, in 1958.

This was the period between his quitting Southern Bell and being given an opportunity with the wise guys in 1959. I had one pair of pants and one pair of shoes in those days. Even so, our mom always tried to keep us looking our best. We were living in houses that my dad could rent if he fixed them up and painted them. It seemed that we were always painting houses that we moved into as a family. That was part of our rent deal.

And the rats. I can also remember the rats. One time we lived in a house that had rats the size of cats, you know, and they'd come out at night, especially. They walked across our living room like it was nothing. I remember throwing golf clubs at them as a kid.

Because we were so poor, we learned how to eat Spam, scrambled eggs, black-eyed peas, grits and Wheatina, which was like Cream of Wheat, and we sprinkled cheese on it. You could buy that mix cheap, and it filled us up. That wasn't so bad, though; even Popeye was eating Wheatina. "I'm strong to da finich, 'cause I eats me ... Wheatina." That was in one of the television commercials. My mother learned all kinds of tricks with Wheatina, but I'd say to her all the time, "Oh, Mother, not Wheatina again tonight."

She'd say, "It's all we have, Thiel." And that's what we ate.

Our family had some very impoverished years before my dad hooked up with the man my mother called "your filthy pseudo-uncle." My preteen years were tough for all of us, but we had a lot of love even in the poor times. We may have eaten eggs every way you can imagine, but my mom and dad made it work even then.

Even though we were poor, my mother always wanted to live in Miami Shores by the bay in Miami, Florida. That was another part of her delusion that she was living a dream, a real fairy tale. Unbelievably, though, her wish did come true one day, but that didn't happen until Uncle Archie came along.

Linda and me in New Jersey.
*"Our mom always tried
to keep us looking our best."*

Mom and Me.

My dad with Linda in New Jersey.

With my Nana in Miami.

Crystal at five years old.

Vonn, my mom, and me
in New Jersey.

CHAPTER SIX

"We have need of a piece of phone equipment for our business,
and we thought you could make it for us."
—Archie Gianunzio, Bookmaker

I n 1958, my father met a wealthy Miami Beach boy by the name
of Ralph Satterfield. Ralph was twenty-five at the time, and my
dad was forty-one. Ralph's aunt was a friend of my dad's, and she
told him she had a nephew who wanted to meet him. Ralph, it
seemed, was fascinated with electronics, and he just couldn't get
enough of my dad's inventions. My father's association with Ralph
plays a huge role in this story. In fact, it may play the biggest role.

Somehow Ralph Satterfield knew that my dad had been badly
treated by corporate America. There would be others who would
mistreat him, and, of course, shrewd businessmen stole from him,
too, but I believe that Southern Bell was the first to try to block my
father's inventions. As it turns out, some of his later inventions
were illegal, and I'm getting to that, but the speakerphone, which
was invented to help the handicapped, was kept from the public
just to block him from realizing the American dream. You see,
people can wait until a patent expires before running with somebody's prototype. My dad never had the money to keep up with
the fees.

Anyway, Ralph must have known something about that. It
seems he had a blood uncle in Manhattan, Sylvester Glazer, a jeweler, and Ralph convinced my dad to go up to New York because
of that connection. Ralph knew that the wise guys used his Uncle
Sylvester to make jewelry for their girlfriends and wives, and he
also knew the mob had the money to make my dad's financial

problems go away. There was no doubt in Ralph's mind that the underworld could use my father's services.

One day, Ralph says, "Listen, my uncle is up in New York, and my other uncle and him own a jewelry store called Sylvester's Jewelry Store. They might be interested in some of these things you can make."

At the time, my father was looking for a solution to help feed his family, and he decided to go up there to see what they had in mind. I have wondered if he had some kind of moral struggle with that before the fact. Nobody forced him to take that step; it was his decision whether or not to go up there. My dad was a good, honest man, but I believe our situation convinced him to take the chance and check it out. I forget where we were living at the time, but there's no doubt that we were in dire financial straits. He knew that helping them out would help us out.

My father made that trip to New York so his kids could eat something other than Wheatina. Right or wrong, I think he saw it that way, and like he'd rationalize years later, "There wasn't any harm done by what I was doing; nobody was getting hurt." I couldn't say the same about my later decision to go down the wrong road, but I'm talking about my father here.

Anyway, my dad says to Ralph, "All right, let's go up there."

Uncle Sylvester could really tell this story back in the day. Probably because Ralph did, I called him Uncle Sylvester, too. Anyway, Ralph and my dad walk into the jewelry store, and Uncle Sylvester says to my dad, "So, you're the maverick genius inventor that my nephew's bragging about?"

Humble as he was, my dad still says, "Yeah, I suppose I am."

"Well, I'd like for you to meet some of my business associates, wealthy businessmen here in Manhattan. I make all their jewelry for them."

"Okay, let's meet 'em," my dad tells him, naively all enthused.

Archie Gianunzio came over to the store to meet my father, and, of course, he liked my dad right away. Archie tells him, "We have need of a piece of phone equipment for our business, and we thought maybe you could make it for us."

"What do you need?" asked my father.

"First of all, we think our phones are being tapped," Archie told him.

"No problem," said my dad. Even back in Capone's day, a guy in the underworld had figured out how to wiretap and bug phones with what they called a cheese box, so my dad sweeps the phone lines at their houses and finds out that their phone lines were being tapped.

My dad asked them, "What do you guys do?"

"We're bookmakers," answered Archie, "and we're not communicating well."

"Gambling bookmakers?"

"Yeah, we do gambling bookmaking," he said.

Joe Valachi was part of that operation, and he was the guy who eventually brought out the FBI by leaking the names of Gianunzio and his associates. In fact, he was the first Mafia member, a soldier in the Genovese crime family, to acknowledge publicly the existence of the Mafia, which he did in 1963 at the McClellan Hearings. Before that, though, Archie Gianunzio becomes my father's newest financial backer, and they go off to this house in Mamaroneck, New York, where Archie's plugged in—a big, beautiful, sprawling house. Archie is a very wealthy man by then—he's got 1100 guys on the street. As a matter of fact, he was the biggest bookmaker in the business at the time, but like he said, his guys were having difficulty communicating.

After my dad fixed it so that phone calls coming into the house weren't being tapped, they wanted him to make it so that the calls could also be dialed *out* without being tapped, and they needed to handle long distance, too. Just like with all of my father's inventions, people were never satisfied with what they asked him to make for them in the first place; they always wanted more.

When my dad made the other equipment they needed, he also worked it so the calls were toll free. They wanted the calls to come in and go out untapped, they wanted toll free long distance, and then they wanted the unit to be portable. That's how the black box happened to be invented in 1959, which was the reason my dad was indicted and called to testify at the McClellan Hearings. At the hearings and in the press they also called the black box a "parasite."

After my dad made the black box, Archie says, "Listen, we also need a piece of equipment that can follow us. Do you think you could give us something like that?"

My dad says, "Yeah, give me a couple of months." He went back to the drawing board, and he designed what he called automatic dial transfer. Remember, if he could draw it, he could make it. They wanted that done for the bookmakers, too. Bookmakers get arrested by using the phone in their house, but if you have the call forwarded, all the cops can do is get the equipment; they're not going to get the bookmaker.

When he made the prototype for call forwarding, Archie said, "Can you make it where we can do it from another phone, Walter?"

My dad said, "Give me another month." And that's when he made it remote.

He called the call forwarding unit "extend-a-call," and the remote dialing apparatus went with that so they could change the number without going back to the office. The numbers could be changed from the bookmaker's house. That's why the feds were getting the equipment by raiding rooms, but they weren't getting the bookmaker.

The "Black Box," invented in 1959.

"A fantastic little device."
Quote from *The Daily Times,* March 28, 1961.

If the bookmakers weren't at home, they could just call the equipment from a pay phone, program the number where they were going to be, and the phone could follow them around the five boroughs of New York City. What they would do was rent an apartment in a fictitious name, put the equipment in there, the equipment could sit dormant in a room, and they'd never have to go to it again. It could be programmed anyplace in the boroughs, and that's how the prototype of call forwarding and the remote dialing apparatus happened to be invented by my father.

My dad corrected the senators at the McClellan Hearings when they called his invention a cheese box, which was the device invented earlier that connected two phones to prevent tracing. The committee asked him about all the extra material that had been purchased to make the cheese boxes. That's when my father made the distinction, and told them that material had been purchased to make other equipment, too.

Senator McClellan said, "In other words, there was other equipment purchased, but the equipment was for something else other than the making of these boxes?"

"Yes, sir," my dad answered him.

"Have we stumbled on what that other equipment is?" McClellan went on.

"They described it as cheese boxes, which is incorrect."

"What is the technical name for them?" asked the chairman.

"Automatic dialing transfer equipment," my dad told him.

"What does the transfer have to do with it? Transfer it around the charge box?"

"No, sir," said my father, "this again is incorrect."

"Would the telephone company know that such a long distance call was being made?"

"Yes, sir," he answered. "It is recorded; it is registered. This equipment would not reflect any complete call. The equipment when it was designed would complete the status of a call and merely transfer it to another station automatically."

Senator McClellan then stated, "In other words, you call from one telephone and the equipment would transfer it to another?"

"With this additional equipment, yes, sir," my father answered. "In other words, a phone call would actually follow you around if you so desired it. This is not a cheese box operation."

"That is the kind where you put it in over here, and if you had another line running, it would transfer to the office downtown or somewhere?" asked the chairman.

And my dad explained to him, "If you were to select or dial in, then with a preconceived telephonic arrangement you could pre-select a coding number on a recorder which would then automatically file the number where you are. This is all done by dial impulses, and also recorder apparatus so that every call that comes in and goes out is automatically recorded."

Again, Senator McClellan asked, "What do you call that?"

"Automatic dial transfer," my dad told him.

Walter L. Shaw invented that back in 1959. He filed for the patent in 1968, and Patent No. 3,591,727 for the Automatic Rerouting System for Telephone Subscriber Station, commonly called call forwarding, was issued to him on July 6, 1971. Did you know that Walter L. Shaw invented the prototype for call forwarding? You didn't know that, did you?

I told a story to *Maxim Magazine* a few years ago. This was back in 2003—March 20, 2003, to be exact—two days before U.S. cruise missiles and bombs were being dropped on Baghdad. I was sitting in the lobby of the St. Regis Hotel in New York City, and I took out a wad of hundred-dollar bills. I put four thousand dollars on the table, and I says, "It's yours if you can find me a single person in this room who can name the man who invented conference calling." I was serious. Of course, no one could name him.

No one can name my father for anything he invented. My father was a great man, and no one knows about him. He was the real thing; I'm just a thief, a nobody, but I'm the one who gets the hype. I'm not denying that I like the hype. I do. But my dad got nothing but jail time.

Like I said earlier, though, I know my father had his cracks. He may have been naïve, but he knew what the wise guys were doing with his inventions. And he knew that what they were doing wasn't right. But the money talked to him. He was broke until he met them, and they gave him five hundred bucks a week to feed his family, and $1,000 to $1,500 per unit for the black box. They even bought my mom and him matching Thunderbirds. Unbelievably, the organization also rented a big, beautiful house for us in Miami Shores. My mother's dream came true, but like I said earlier, it didn't last long.

CHAPTER SEVEN

*"You have your father's genes; you
could have done anything you put your mind to."*
—Betty Lou Shaw

When my dad decided to stay and help the wise guys in New York, we all lived at the Grand Concourse Hotel across from Yankee Stadium. That's where I met Ralph Satterfield for the first time. That's where I met everybody for the first time—Joe Valachi being one of them. I met Archie Gianunzio at the Grand Concourse Hotel, too. I called him Uncle Archie, just like Uncle Sylvester, but Archie was my so-called "filthy pseudo-uncle." I found out years later that he was the one paying for us to stay in that fancy hotel.

Anyway, my first attempt at conning went down with Archie Gianunzio. Uncle Sylvester had given me some fake jewelry; he had some junk in his jewelry store, too. He told me it was costume jewelry, not the real stuff, just some cuff links that he couldn't sell. The cuff links had fake stones and all that nonsense in them. I knew they weren't real, Sylvester told me that, but I wanted to try the guy on. I wanted to see if this guy, Archie, would bite.

So I was meeting Archie Gianunzio for the first time in the lobby of the Grand Concourse Hotel. I showed the cuff links to him, and, of course, he knew they came from Sylvester's. I didn't know their connection to one another at that point. Archie says to me, "Oh, we've got a little entrepreneur here. How much do you want for these, kid?" He knew what I was doing, and I'm an eleven-year-old kid doing that!

I told him I wanted fifty bucks, and he pulled out this wad that would choke a horse. I'd never seen anything like it. He gives me the fifty, and I said, "Just like that?"

And he said, "It's nothing. What's fifty bucks, kid?"

So Uncle Archie was my first fence. That was the first jewelry I ever owned, and I wanted to see if he'd buy it off me. I never expected him to give me the money, but when I went back to the store, I told Sylvester that I'd sold the cuff links to Archie for fifty dollars.

"You did what? He knows they're junk."

"You think so?" I asked him.

"He's been buying jewelry here for his girlfriend for as long as I can remember. Of course he knows they're junk. He was just playing with you because he likes your dad."

Ralph Satterfield had an MG convertible, and he would come over to the hotel at night and take me out for ice cream. And when my dad found a place to live in Westchester, Uncle Archie would take me into the city for ice cream. It was cold in New York, but we would go to Howard Johnson's in Manhattan and eat ice cream together. One time, we even met Eddie Burns. Archie knew him. Eddie played the part of Kookie on a TV show called *77 Sunset Strip*. I was just a little kid then, and I thought Archie was the nicest guy in the world.

I thought all those guys were it, you know. And my mother saw that right away. She saw the danger signs all over. I was exposed to the wise guys early on, and I was fascinated with all of it. I can remember smelling their colognes at the hearings later on, and they were all wearing big watches and fancy jewelry. My dad's side of the family was Sicilian, but that had nothing to do with my fascination with them. Not even knowing what it was all about or what they really did, I was enthralled with them from the very beginning.

You know, that's sad to me now. I had no interest in what my dad was making at our kitchen table, but I couldn't get enough of those guys. Uncle Archie even gave me a little black trench coat, and I wore that every place I went until I couldn't wear it anymore.

I had no interest in school, either. Even in the early grades I was failing everything. I actually failed first grade twice. It isn't an exaggeration to say that I failed everything I did in school. When I dropped out at seventeen, I should have been in twelfth grade, but I was still in grade ten. Just like my dad, I didn't even make it through high school. He dropped out in the ninth grade, and I only passed through the tenth—the genius and the flunky.

It wasn't that I felt like a flunky; I knew I had the capability to do well if I tried; I just wasn't willing to work at it. I didn't like school. I thought it was boring; everything we were learning was mundane. I didn't even like reading. Nothing appealed to me. Here my dad was brilliant in mathematics, electronics, engineering and all that, and I was a horrible student. I'll say it again that I was his opposite. It's funny, though: I never thought about that. I never thought to myself that I could never do what he did. I never wanted to do what he could do. Nothing about what he was doing interested me. My genes were very different from my dad's, but my mother didn't think so.

When I was in prison, I can remember her saying, "You have your father's genes, and you could have done anything you wanted to do. You could have been a great attorney, Thiel. Anything you wanted to do, you could have done, but you chose what you thought was the easy road—the fast, quick buck." She was right about that. I have always wanted things to happen fast. I thought about being a trial lawyer, but that was going to take too long.

They say I got the quick fix over 2,000 times in my career. I don't know how many times I've read that. Did I tell that to somebody? I might ask you how many times you brushed your teeth last week. You might say twenty-one. Did you brush any more, any less? Might have been more, could have been less. Why don't you remember? You haven't kept track. Why haven't you kept track? Because it wasn't important to keep track. That's why I didn't keep track of our burglaries.

A school photo at the age of twelve or thirteen.

It wasn't about the numbers after a while. It was just a job, and there's no quick fix in jewel thievery anyway; it's all about knowing what you're doing and being consistent about it. If you're not consistent, there's no quick fix, and it could cost you life in prison. Anyway, I never kept track of how many robberies I committed. I want to keep that in my rearview mirror, behind me.

Back to when my dad was staying in New York, I was failing everything back home in Florida. My mother preferred being in Florida, and Linda didn't want to be away from her high school friends, so my mother, Linda, Crystal, and I were back in Miami. It seemed, though, that my parents thought it might help my school situation for me to be in the North with my father. But my mother said, "There is only one way I'll let Thiel stay up there with you, and that's if you put him in a private school. I want him isolated from all those people you're dealing with. I don't want him anywhere near them."

Being the little kid that I was, however, they had lied to me saying that Archie and the rest of them were accountants. Mobsters or accountants, it made no difference to me. My mom saw what was happening, and she didn't like it. "Don't you see what's happening to your son?" she'd ask my father. "Today he wears a trench coat. Tomorrow he'll carry a gun."

The whole Ralph Satterfield/Uncle Archie thing makes for a great story. I loved them both, and they had something to do with the way I turned out, especially Archie. But I don't want this book to be another Mafia story. I mean, who cares? The gig is up. The mob is broken. It's dismantled, and it's no longer "organized." There's no great organized crime syndicate anymore. It's over.

When I was part of it, there were probably 21,000 members, and it must be down to less than 700 now. It wasn't so much the law that broke them down; I think that drugs, greed and breaking the rules of the old guard—calling us dinosaurs and Moustache

Pete's—that's what broke us down. The structure was very solid at one time, and I think it got watered down with each new generation. They just threw the wheels away, just got to be cowboys and rats. It became too easy to turn a guy who was facing hard time, and that's what broke it down. It fell apart from the inside out.

There are still a handful of wise guys out there. I'm an old moustache. I'm the old line of not earning off of lives of drugs and prostitution. Don't make money just any old way. I'm talking about earning. I didn't earn off of somebody's pain. But that's hypocritical: I made some good money extorting, and I stole a lot of beautiful things that probably meant something to rich people. Extortion was one thing, but taking jewelry from the rich never seemed like it was hurting anybody.

There are lots of guys who can write stories about the old wise guy days. I'll say it again: This story is about a father and a son. What made me become a germ? That's really what this is about: What made me become a mutant? What made me a monster coming from such a gifted human being as my father? What happened to me? I go back to saying Frankenstein was born in the Old Senate Office Building in Washington, D.C.

Like my mother said, I came from a home where there was love, but I still became a criminal. You choose one way or another in your formative years. You twist and turn as a kid. Archie used to say to me, "Kids are very impressionable. They are easy to sway." I didn't have to be swayed. Wearing that trench coat, I was just a kid, but I already thought I was one of them. In the not too distant future, I had to learn the hard way that *I wasn't them yet.*

CHAPTER EIGHT

"That's when I started hating rich people."
Walter T. Shaw

I t wasn't that I wanted to leave my mother to go to New Jersey, but she thought I might do better in a private school near my dad. Trying to get me excited, they told me, "We're going to put you in a school where you'll be riding horses. It's a military school."

My dad told me he'd come and see me every weekend, and he promised I could go home to Miami on vacations. Like I said, my mom and dad weren't separated. She just wasn't staying up there in the cold weather, and his business associates didn't want him far away. They wanted him where they could watch him. He was making a product for them, and because they were investing in my dad, they had control of his whereabouts.

Anyway, I remember the day I went to Oakland Military Academy in Oakland, New Jersey, for the first time. I can see all of it. Just like they promised, there were horses there, and I loved horses. Looking back, I was glad to be part of that. Compared to the way we'd been living for so many years, I loved what was offered there. I enjoyed the clothes and dressing up for school and chow. I had no problem with being there, but things didn't always go smoothly with some of the kids.

Anyway, in 1959, 1960 and 1961, my dad's making the black boxes, and I'm seeing him and Archie when I can. I'm going down to Sylvester's store with my dad on my breaks and weekends. Very faithfully, he was picking me up, and we would spend time together. Looking back, my fondest memories of time spent with my dad are those days in New York City. We used to walk all over Manhattan together looking for electronics parts for his inventions. To this day, New York is my favorite city. Then it all ended one Friday afternoon, March 31, 1961.

I was all dressed up and waiting for my dad to come and get me. Earlier that day, the headmaster brought two men over to see me. He says, "Walter, these men are here to see you." I'm thirteen years old at the time, just a kid.

One of them asks me, "Is your dad coming today?"

"Yeah, he's coming," I told him. "He comes every weekend."

They told me they were friends of his, so they would wait for my father to arrive. The two of them looked nothing like the friends of his I knew, and they sat waiting for him in a blue Ford sedan. I learned later, of course, that they were really FBI agents. Pretty soon, I saw my dad's black Lincoln Continental pull in; then I saw the car pull out and race away. The feds caught my dad and Archie, but I didn't know that then.

Instead of letting me go back to my room that day, the head-master put me all alone in the school's infirmary. He told me that my mother would be calling; they couldn't discuss it with me. So I'm in there wondering why. What have I done to be in the infir-mary? Am I sick? That night, my mother gets on the phone and tells me I'm coming home. I was thrilled about that, but I still wasn't getting it.

When I found the courage to ask her what had happened, she says, "Your father got involved with that filthy man you call Uncle Archie. Of course, your dad is innocent, but the law doesn't know that. He's hanging around them all the time. You can't trust peo-ple, Thiel, and your father's finding that out the hard way."

The next morning, my friend slips *The New York Times* under the door. The headlines were all about my father and Uncle Archie, and all these guys being arrested. They were calling them members of the "Mafia." My dad was listed right there in the article. I've still got the newspaper clipping framed on my wall. It said that he'd been arrested and placed in jail—a criminal, charged with unlawfully attaching a device to a Bell Telephone line. I was in total shock.

I could hear the kids laughing outside the infirmary door that day, and one of them says, "I told you his dad was doing something wrong." They never thought I was one of them, a doctor or a lawyer's son. There was something different about me. I wasn't polished like them.

Those kids wouldn't have been tough guys if I hadn't been locked up in a cold, quiet room with nothing in it. It was just like the cell I landed in years later, not even a window. I spent the whole weekend alone in there, waiting for somebody to rescue me. Those were the longest days of my life, and that's when I started hating rich people. Oakland was for rich kids, a bunch of aristocrats.

When the headmaster locked me up in the infirmary, all shut in like I was a disease, I saw how the wealthy are. For the first time, I got a sense of them. I was isolated in that room, separated from the others, and then I was thrown out. They were rich, and I wasn't. Because my dad had been arrested, I was beneath them. I really believe that was my first experience with hating the rich. It wouldn't be my last.

I wasn't blaming anyone but my dad for what happened, though, and I was angry at him. What was he really doing with those guys? Was he lying to me? Archie was supposed to be an accountant. In retrospect, I would have done the same thing if I was him, and I did one day.

When I had kids of my own, I never wanted them to know what I was doing for a living. That should say something right there. My first wife would say to me, "How many years are you going to keep doing this? You don't need to keep robbing houses. It's over. You're set for life." I told her I would stop when Shelly, our little girl, asked for accountability.

"I'll quit then, I promise you," I told her.

The moment of truth came while we were all in the car one night. Shelly says to me, "We have a thing in school, Daddy, where we're supposed to say what our fathers do at work. What do you do at work?"

My wife leaned over on her elbow in my Cadillac, and I'll never forget it, she says, "Well, the moment of truth is here. What are you going to tell your daughter that you do?"

I told Shelly I owned a clothing store. I did own a clothing store, but nothing I was doing was legal. Extortion is probably the worst thing I have ever done to people to make money, but I didn't lie to my daughter by telling her I owned a clothing store. I just hadn't gone about ownership the right way.

Her mother shook her head and said, "You didn't answer the way I thought you would." She thought I'd tell the truth to our daughter, but I couldn't do it. What was I going to tell my little girl? I reasoned that I was doing the same thing my dad had done to me. He lied to spare me as a kid, and I did the same thing. I had no idea what was happening the day my dad's car raced away from the academy.

The next day, nobody came for me. Instead, unbelievably, I took the Greyhound bus home by myself from Oakland, New Jersey, to Miami, Florida. That was 1,112 miles—the longest ride of my life after the longest days of my life. The headmaster let me take only the clothes I was wearing, and the rich boys weren't sorry to see me go.

I was skinny, frail and sickly as a little kid. I had all kinds of ear and throat troubles, which started during our time on Elmendorf Air Force Base in Alaska, but the weather in New Jersey was not kind to me, either. Maybe ninety pounds by the age of twelve, I had to make myself tough.

Even before he was arrested, there had been rumors at the academy about my father being a gangster, and when somebody said something like that, I took them on. I wasn't afraid of any-body; I even broke a kid's jaw one time. I was trying to be a tough guy, but they kicked the shit out of me there.

My dad had drummed it into me as a kid that there was no shame in falling down or getting knocked down; the shame was in not getting up. "They can knock you down a hundred times, but you get back up," he told me. I would take on guys bigger than me all the time, and I didn't care about the consequences.

I had to grow up fast and start taking a lot of crap when my dad ran into trouble. At that point, I was fighting back. I didn't like what those rich kids had said to me, and I didn't like the fact that I was thrown out of a prestigious military school. I was out of their school, out of their league. But I would later find a way into their big houses.

My mother said to me when I got home, "What did you expect? You were in with the bluebloods. You thought they were going to accept you after your father's arrest? They don't get arrested."

CHAPTER NINE

"Never open your mouth, and you'll never get into trouble."
—Archie Gianunzio, Bookmaker

I'm jumping years ahead to the early 1970s, but it seems important to explain here what happened that day in 1961. My dad
and I got into a fight one time, a verbal exchange, and he says,
"You know, Thiel, you've always admired those guys and the
lifestyle they represent. I'm telling you, they're all traitors. But
you're not going to believe me. I know that. If you want the truth
about what happened with me that day you were left waiting at the
academy, go see Archie. You tell him to tell you the truth," he told
me. "He'll know what that means." That wasn't the first time my
dad had said something like that, and it seemed like the right time
to do what he suggested.

One of my best friends and I went to Archie's diner in
Westchester, New York, Chat 'n' Chew. There he was sitting at a
table, gray-haired by then. Early on, I had always known him as
being quite thin with black hair. His face was pockmarked, but he
was still a nice looking man in his early sixties. Anyway, he's sitting
in the diner with his spectacles on his nose, and he's reading the
racing form. I remember him looking at the door. He sees me, and
motions me over.

When I get to the table, Archie says, "I recognize the walk. I
don't recognize the kid, but I'd recognize the walk anywhere."

I walk just like my dad did. I never tried to do that, I just do.
My father had a real fast gait, and my mother told me I walked like
him ever since I was a little kid. Maybe I imitated him one time
and it stuck. That must be it.

Hi, kid, how are you doing?" Archie asks me.

"Good, Uncle Archie," I told him.

"What brings you to my neck of the woods? Miami's a long way from Westchester."

I told him my dad sent me to see him. That's when he said, "We've come a long way from the Grand Concourse Hotel and fake jewelry."

"Yes, we have," I agreed. Until that moment at the diner, I had never heard a word from him about that.

Trying to make light of things, he asks, "Where's the trench coat?"

I smiled then told him again that my dad had sent me to see him. Archie knew it would all come back on him one day. Sooner or later, I would be my own man. When we look at things as a kid, we bounce with them. They aren't magnified until we look back. Archie knew there would come a time that I would want to get to the bottom of things. You know, why did my dad get arrested the day I was waiting for him at the academy? That had never come out. How would the FBI have known that he was making things for the wise guys? Who would have told that to them?

"So, I see 'truth day' has come," he says. That's what he called it.

Remember, at the age of eleven I had my first walk with Archie to get ice cream at Howard Johnson's. We were walking down the pier, and he says, "You see those fish they caught? You know how they got there?"

I said to him, "No, how did they get there Uncle Archie?"

"They opened their mouths. Never open your mouth and you will never get into trouble. You don't want somebody to know something that could hurt you."

Of course, my mother had always warned me about the same thing. "They'll know your dirt and tell people. If you don't want your thoughts told, get close to nobody," she cautioned me.

I liked the way Archie said the same thing, so I always used to say that: "I'm not a fish. I'm never going to open my mouth." I mean, it was a standing joke with us. Archie was the one who told me that.

Any time I came out with those things as a kid, my dad would ask, "Where'd you hear that?" I'd tell him Archie told me. It was Archie this and Archie that, you know, and it used to wear on my parents. But Archie's early warning was behind my belief in being a stand-up kind of guy. I wasn't talking to nobody.

So that day in the diner, I says, "What do you mean, 'truth day'? What are you going to tell me?"

He answered me, "You want to know why your father got arrested; am I right?"

"Yeah, I want to know that," I told him. "How could the feds target my dad? How did they know what he was doing?"

Archie looks at me and says, "Walter, listen to me." Then he starts telling me the story. "You remember the day we drove off from your school when the feds were there? Well, kid, the police were there, too."

"I know that, Archie."

"They did what cops do: They separated us. They separate you when you get arrested to see who is going to crack first."

I tell him, "My dad's not going to say nothing. And you're not going to say nothing. You always told me never to open my mouth."

"I know. He didn't say anything," he agrees with me, "but there is more to the story."

"So what are you saying to me?" I ask him.

"They told me your dad had a heart attack and died during the interrogation. In their words they said, 'Mr. Shaw had a heart attack and died in his cell.'"

"So?"

He says, "Well, I thought he was dead, so there was no harm in talking about a dead man."

He might have concocted that story. We'll never know whether it's true or not, but that's the story Archie passed to me. Right there he admitted that he told the authorities my dad was making the black box, and my dad was indicted for that. He was charged with unlawfully attaching a device to a Bell Telephone line.

"Why didn't the organization kill you for talking like that?" I asked him. Under the old code of guards, it wouldn't have mattered what the police had told Archie; it wasn't enough to open his mouth.

"Funny thing is, because they care about your dad so much, they did want to kill me, but he wouldn't hear of it."

"Really," I said, amazed by that.

"Actually, kid, I did die. They did the next best thing. I was stripped of my position for doing that. They gave me ten men and threw me out." As I said earlier, Archie had 1100 guys on the street when I met him. His bookmaking operations did $10 million a year, which breaks down to $30,000 a day!

Uncle Archie broke my heart that day in the diner. "I built my whole life around what you were supposed to be," I told him. "Way back on that pier, I was a little kid, and you said to me, 'Never open your mouth, and you'll never get into trouble.' And you're telling me you didn't stand up?"

"I thought he was dead, Walter."

"I guess we won't be taking any more walks with ice cream cones," I told him. Archie Gianunzio was my first major disappointment in the underworld.

Archie told me something else that day. He says, "Let me tell you a story about the kind of man your dad is. I had this girl come in, and I took a bet with all of my men that this broad couldn't get your father to have dinner with her under any pretense."

"So what'd you do?"

I told her, "You get this guy to have dinner with you, and I'll give you a new Cadillac, a mink coat, and a diamond ring. That's all you gotta do, get him to have dinner with you."

He puts my dad at the counter in the diner, and the girl is two seats down. They are sitting there, and she finally makes chit chat with him. They exchanged names, and she says, "What are you doing up here?"

He tells her, "I live up here, and my partner's up here."

"How would you like to have dinner with me?" she offers.

"Oh, no, I couldn't do that. I'm married."

"I know you're married. I'm not asking you to go to bed with me; I'm just asking you to have dinner."

"No, I couldn't do that," he tells her again.

That went on for a while, and finally the girl told him the truth. She told him she was getting a Cadillac, a mink coat, and a diamond ring if she could get him to have dinner with her. He says, "Well, I'd like to help you out, but here's the problem. I'm married, my wife's in Florida, and if anybody saw us eating in this restaurant together, it would break her heart. I wouldn't want that on my conscience, so I have to respectfully decline." The girl came back and told Archie about the conversation.

Archie said, "That's the kind of man your father was, kid. He was never one of us, and we knew we were never going to be one of him." The wise guys loved my dad. He was like that white spot in a dark crowd. You know what I mean?

After meeting with Archie, I got off the plane in Florida, and I drove to my dad's house. He was living in another rental in Miami Shores at the time. I told him, "I saw Archie."

He asked me, "And what happened?"

I said, "Truth day."

"Broke your heart, huh?"

"Yeah. Do you believe he gave you up?"

He says, "Yeah, I believe he was sacrificing me for his wellbeing. I was expendable. He knew he wouldn't get recourse from me. I wasn't a wise guy. I wasn't going to order his death. I could have, but he knew I wouldn't. I was never one of them. They're all like that. They'll give you up if it helps them. You don't want to hear that, do you, Thiel?"

"I did hear it," I tell him.

He says, "Well, I've been trying to tell you, but it took Archie to get it through to you. 'Truth day' he calls it. It's about time he told you the truth."

I reminded my dad that the boss wanted to kill Archie over that. I don't remember who the boss was at the time, but he knew my dad had stood up. I learned that the boss called my dad to a meeting, and he asked him, "What do you want us to do, Walter?"

"Don't do anything for me. Not like that. I don't live my life that way," my dad says to him.

My father never looked at himself as being anything other than an inventor, but when I was going down that road, I would say, "Dad, you weren't just an inventor to them. You were known as an associate."

He told me, "They can look at me any way they want. I made something for them, and I'll have to live with that the rest of my life. I got mixed up with those people for the money. It was the money, Thiel. I don't think the way they do. I'm not like them."

"You live in the gray, Dad, and there is no gray. It's black or white. You're either in or you're not. You can't be half pregnant," I said. "I won't be half pregnant. I'll get my own name, my own reputation, and I'm going to go into the ocean and swim to the other side. I'm not coming back to shore."

"If you're going that way, then I guess I have no son."

The saddest part of this story for me is that he was right. For almost thirty years, we were estranged. He just kept getting screwed, and I was looking for revenge. In my dad's life, he had no father. In mine, I went "that way," and my father had no son.

CHAPTER TEN

"Try to go forth and sin no more."
—Senator John L. McClellan

After being thrown out of Oakland Military Academy, things changed in a big way in Miami. In the weeks that followed my dad's arrest, the Thunderbirds were sold, and movers showed up to transport our stuff from Miami Shores to a modest ranch-style house in Ives Estates. That was a real step down on the other side of Miami. We were living about a block from the bay in a beautiful house at the time.

The mob also sent a guy named Tony to live with my mother and my sisters, Linda and Crystal. Of course, I showed up in Miami soon after my dad's arrest, and I was wondering where Tony popped up from. He was a good looking guy, in the Navy stationed in Florida, and he was also a bookmaker. As a favor to that relationship, they asked him to stay in our house while my dad was out on bond in New York with Uncle Archie. They were keeping an eye on my mom. By Tony living there, he was listening to the kinds of conversations that were coming up and all that. They needed to make sure there wasn't any talk of my dad making a deal. In other words, Tony was there to protect the wise guys, not my father or his family. That was the edge they held at my dad's throat.

The story about my dad was all over the papers in Miami, too, and I found that out when my mother sent me off to Ives Elementary School. On my first day, the full force of the sixth grade gang confronted me during recess. Gary Butts, Bob "French" Clark, and Russell Kane were the ringleaders. They were all calling my father a thug and a gangster. I knew he wasn't a gangster, and I was quick to tell them so. Just like my fights at the academy, though, I got the shit kicked out of me the first day at Ives.

At school the next day, it looked like it was going to start all over again. Instead, French Clark said to the crowd gathered around us, "He ain't no sissy." From then on, I was almost a celebrity, a real hero. I would laugh when my dad was called a criminal, but I was still real mad at him on the inside, not getting what was really going on.

When my father got out on bond up there, he was restricted to New York. Because the same charge had been filed against him in Florida, unlawfully attaching a device to a Bell telephone line, he couldn't come home anyway. I'll get into that later. He called my mother every night, but I wouldn't speak to him. My behavior went downhill from the minute my mother had me back in Miami. She always said I was a different kid when I got off that Greyhound bus from Oakland.

I had proved myself to the tough gang at school, though, and I was going to be tougher than any of them. I stayed out at night doing all kinds of bad things with Russell, French and Gary. We stole ice cream, bicycles and all that nonsense. It is fair to say that I was always in trouble in the neighborhood.

Even back then, I had a real mean streak in me, wanting to get back at somebody or something for what was happening to my family. There was a little ice cream parlor in the neighborhood, and I'd show off my bravery and daring by stealing ice cream right in front of the old lady working there. I'd go back to the freezer and stuff popsicles and ice cream under my jacket. Then I'd go right up to the old lady at the counter and say, "You don't see any ice cream on me, do you?" Scared to death, she'd always deny seeing anything. I loved to do that with my gang.

One incident, in particular, stands out. We were running through Ives Estates, and I spotted a nice bike that a kid had gotten for Christmas. It was a brand-new bright red Schwinn bicycle with skirts, and I lifted it. I said, "Let's take it." So Gary Butts and I took it. I painted it with metallic blue paint, and we took the skirts off to change it up a bit. The thing is, though, it had a skip in the chain. The kid's parents were planning to return it after Christmas for a new one, and that would be the dead giveaway that it was his bike.

I happened to have a beef with a kid in our gang by the name of Danny Cooper. We never got along. I was a leader, and he wasn't. So he starts telling people where the bike is, and the cops come knocking on Gary's and my door. That was my first experience with the cops, and I didn't like it. I also learned never to do anything with anybody I couldn't trust. Gary, I could trust; Gary stood up. But I go back to my mother's advice: "If you don't trust them, they can't hurt you." Nobody else should have known about that bike.

Then again, I had a father who later said to me, "I never met a man I didn't like." Opposing viewpoints. I went with my mother's way of thinking.

So the cops knocked on the door, and they says, "We know this is So-and-so's bike."

My mom says, "How do you know that?" Looking back on it, though, she must have been wondering where that bike had come from.

I was hiding out in my room, but I remembered something Archie had told me: "Always remain calm, kid. Don't let anybody see that you're upset."

With that in mind, I decided to come to the doorway, and the cops told me to ride the bike for them. So I ride the bike, and it had a skip in it. Then they said, "That's how we know. Do you notice that skip? It's a malfunction, the kid's parents told us about it, and the bike was lifted. We will not prosecute your son if you make good on the bike." Gary's and my dad had to buy the kid a new bike.

I couldn't go outside for a month after that, and neither could Gary. I may have been running wild around the neighborhood and all that, but I was disciplined as a kid. My dad wasn't going to let me get away with that. After the bicycle incident, he insisted that I talk to him on the phone. All the way from New York, he says, "You're punished. You're in the house, and now you gotta watch your little sister all the time."

When he chastised me for stealing, I remember asking him if he was inventing illegal communications devices: "Is that how you're making your money?"

He says to me, "If you want to make excuses for all the wrong you've been doing by making me out to be some kind of criminal, the decision is yours. Things haven't been easy for us, but what's your mother doing? Is she robbing grocery stores to feed you?" That's a twist when I think of it. In my adult life, I have justified all the trashy things I've done by painting him as a saint that got screwed. I wasn't getting it as a kid.

Eventually, I wasn't even going to school anymore, and my mother knew I was in big trouble. Even when I was a kid, she could see that I was going down the wrong road. When my mom couldn't handle me anymore, my dad took a chance on being arrested in Florida by leaving New York. He just appeared at our house one night. Nobody told me he was coming. I didn't know until I saw the taxi outside the front door. Simple as it sounds, I remember thinking, *Oh, boy, something's about to happen.* I guess I've always been juiced when something's about to go down.

He came inside that night and said, "Thiel, we tried you with your mother, and it didn't work. Now you're coming with me to Washington, D.C. You're going to be bored silly, but you're coming with me. This is the way it's going to be." So I got packed and left home with him the following day.

That's when my dad and the others had received a subpoena requiring them to testify at the United States Senate's Permanent

Subcommittee on Investigations hearings on gambling and organized crime, which were chaired by Senator John L. McClellan and were known as the McClellan Hearings. I remember my mother screaming and running around the house when she heard that. She kept saying that Bobby Kennedy was behind it. "Your father's trusting those people got him involved in that!" she screamed. In other words, my dad's innocent in her mind. Mr. Robert F. "Bobby" Kennedy had been the chief counsel of the 1957-1959 Senate Labor Rackets Committee under Chairman McClellan.

My father and I were staying in a nice hotel in Washington, and on weekends, he took me to all the museums and other places tourists go. It was summertime, and he tried to make it like a school trip or something.

I remember asking, "Dad, what are we doing here?"

"I have to go to a big place and answer a bunch of questions," he told me.

I started writing this book by telling about my week in the Old Senate Office Building in 1961. It seemed massive to me as a kid. It was August, too hot for my black trench coat. I was wearing pants and a short sleeve shirt, and my dad was dressed in his one and only suit. People were coming and going, and it was just like a movie in my eyes. To tell you the truth, even the memory is like a movie to me.

When we arrived in Washington, I knew I would see Archie again for the first time in probably six months, and I was ecstatic about that. When he appeared at the hearings, however, Archie was very different towards us, and I couldn't understand it. I realized later that he wasn't there for a reunion; he was there because of a subpoena. Archie had a lot on his mind, including what I now know was his betrayal of my father. He was distant, and I remember him and my dad going off in a corner. They would talk out of earshot, and I was wondering why.

I said to my dad, "How come Archie won't come over here much?"

"Well, he's got a lot on his mind, Thiel. This is not a happy time for any of us. We're not here for pleasure; we're here to answer a bunch of tough questions, and it's not going to be nice."

All this time I'm still thinking they're all innocent. Obviously, I didn't know all the guys in the organization. Archie always introduced them to me as acquaintances, business associates. In my young mind, they weren't the bad guys. They were just old men to me. I was thirteen, and these guys were in their forties and fifties. Very powerful guys. You could tell they were of Archie's league. Just the way they carried themselves, you could see that.

Like I said, Carlo Gambino made a big impression on me. Valachi was in a separate place; he wouldn't come around us. I didn't know he had turned, and I wouldn't have known what it meant, either. Turns out, Valachi was a fish.

When Archie did come talk to me I asked him, "Is Mr. Valachi going to come talk to us?" You'll remember that I had met him at the Grand Concourse Hotel.

Archie said, "He's not coming over here. In fact, we won't see him again."

"Why?"

"We just won't," he tells me. He didn't let me know he'd gone bad. He just said, "It is what it is."

So, Valachi, Gambino, Archie, Joseph Bonanno and several other guys were there. They were all wise guys, and I would find that out later. At the time, though, I was just a kid, and they were all heroes to me. I couldn't wait to be one of them. Rather than being fascinated with what would go down as something historic happening in that Senate building, I was captivated by some of the underworld's most notorious figures.

The one nice thing Uncle Archie did say was just what I wanted to hear: "The government is just jealous of us Italians, kid. They hate us because they know we build empires, and they're scared we're gonna take their country away from them. This is just a conspiracy against Italians, and they're trying to lock us all up." My name might have been Scottish, but I was real proud to be an Italian that day.

Archie was questioned by the committee right before it was my dad's turn. Senator McClellan started out by asking, "Will you give us your name, your place of residence, and your business or occupation?"

"My name is Archie Gianunzio. I live at 236 Union Avenue, Mamaroneck, New York."

"You are in business, are you?" asks the chairman.

And Archie says, "I refuse to answer on the grounds that the answer may tend to incriminate me."

"Are you out of business?" the chairman asks him.

"I was told by my attorney to refuse to answer questions other than my name and my address on the grounds they may tend to incriminate me."

"Are you under indictment at the present time?"

"Sir, I was told to answer two questions, which I answered. I must answer this one in the same manner, that I cannot answer on the grounds it may tend to incriminate me," Archie says again.

He said that nine more times, and Senator McClellan said, "All right, you may stand aside. Call the next witness."

So Mr. Adlerman, the general counsel, said, "Mr. Shaw."

It was brutal when my dad was up there being questioned. Senator McClellan and Mr. Adlerman questioned him. Bobby Kennedy was no longer chief counsel then. He was on his way to being attorney general for his soon-to-be-president, brother, John F. Kennedy. Bobby Kennedy would sometimes walk around the courtroom, though, very arrogant, better than everybody else. It's like he didn't breathe the same air we were breathing. He was on the up and rise.

*Archie Gianunzio testifies at the McClellan Hearings
on August 25, 1961.*
(AP Images)

The organization wouldn't even give my father a lawyer in D.C., so his attorney in Florida was advising him. On the first day he was called to testify at the hearings, Friday, August 25, 1961, he started out by saying, "Before we go into this, I would like to make a request. My attorney was not able to accompany me here. I wonder if it would be possible to have it postponed until he could arrive."

"Where is he now?" asked Senator McClellan.

"At present, it is hard for me to say. I really don't know. The last I heard he was in Mexico," my dad tells him.

"You want us to wait until he returns?"

"Well, I understand he will be back this weekend. I called his law office," he answered.

"Then would you like to return here Monday at your own expense?" said McClellan.

"Yes, sir," my dad agreed.

On Monday, August 28, 1961, Mr. Adlerman called on my father again. Then Senator McClellan asked, "Do you have counsel today?"

"My attorney was not able to appear. He suggested that since there is a pending situation in Miami, Florida, I should not answer any questions," said my dad.

"Are you under indictment?"

"Yes, sir," my dad told him.

"Why is your attorney not here?"

"Well, he had some other business to take care of that he had not finished prior to the time he left," he answered.

"Since he could not come, you have elected not to secure other counsel?" asked Senator McClellan.

"No, sir, I have not elected. I am unable to elect."

"You are unable to elect?" he asked my father. "Do you mean you don't have money to provide other counsel?"

"That is correct," my dad said.

"Is that the reason that your lawyer is not here, because you did not have the money? Is that the principal reason, or because he just got back from a vacation?"

"I do not know, sir," said my dad.

"I think you would have an idea. Have you paid him a fee to be here?"

"No, sir," my dad admitted.

My dad never had any money, and Grandpa Roberts had given him the money for us to stay in the hotel there.

"Very well," said Senator McClellan. "We are going to ask you some questions, and we will try not to trespass upon a privilege that is yours. If you desire—it is a matter that addresses itself to you—if you can't make an honest statement to the effect that you think an answer might tend to incriminate you, if you state that under oath, that you honestly believe it, this committee will respect it."

So the chairman and the general counsel started asking him questions, and he was trying to answer them to the best of his ability. After he admitted to being the inventor of the black box, Mr. Adlerman asked my father, "Did you hear the testimony of the assistant district attorney for Westchester County, Mr. Arthur Spring, the other day at these hearings?"

"Yes, sir," my father told him.

"Did you hear his statement that you were financed on the manufacture of this type of equipment by Mr. Gianunzio, a well-known gambler in Westchester County? I would like to know, having heard that testimony, do you want to make any comment on it?"

"I heard the testimony," said my dad.

"Do you want to make any comment on it?"

"No, sir," my father answered.

"If he commented on it, such comment as he might make might tend to incriminate him, so I am going to respect his position in that area of the testimony," said Senator McClellan.

And my dad says, "Thank you." Right there, he stood up for Archie, who I learned later had betrayed him. Archie was the one bankrolling his manufacture of the black boxes. He was buying the units from my father, but then he leased them out at a weekly rate, which is how he made his income off of the boxes.

When it was all over, I asked my dad, "Why didn't you answer all their questions?"

He told me, "Well, I just can't answer them, Thiel."

"If you're innocent, why can't you?"

He says, "I was told that I can't."

At the time, I didn't understand the power behind who was telling him that. I was getting a picture in my mind, though, that there was some kind of conspiracy going on against the Italians. It seemed that the government was against us: my mother and dad, Uncle Archie, all the other so-called "Mafiosi," and me. Nobody could be trusted. I just wasn't gettin' it.

CHAPTER ELEVEN

"What did you expect from greasy, dirty-blooded Italians?"
—Grandma and Grandpa Roberts

S enator McClellan had said to my father, "Try to go forth and sin no more." What sin was my dad committing? My father was innocent, in my view. But after testifying at the hearings, he still had to stay out of Florida due to a warrant for his arrest there. In Florida, he was charged with using unauthorized equipment on a telephone, a misdemeanor. In New York, he was charged with being part of a controlled gambling syndicate by allegedly selling his equipment to bookmakers, a felony, but those charges were dropped because of the indictment in Florida.

It is important here to explain how the Florida case was built against my father, and this all goes back to Ralph Satterfield again. I'm telling you, Ralph plays a big role in our story. Anyway, the Florida case was based on evidence collected by Dade County State Attorney Richard Gerstein.

I had heard different versions of this story, but I never really read about it until I went looking for newspaper articles on the subject. On August 25, 1961, *The Miami News* ran a story about my dad's being questioned at the McClellan Hearings. That article told all about how he happened to be arrested in Florida back in 1959. That would have been while I was at Oakland Military Academy. Parts of the article read as follows:

"A Miami private detective reported that a man named Ralph Satterfield came to him a year ago saying he knew where he could buy a gadget that would enable him to make free long-distance calls. Satterfield said he was representing Walter Shaw, whom he described as a disgruntled former telephone company installer who went on his own after the telephone company claimed the inventions he had developed with its equipment belonged to the company.

"The private eye said he pretended to go along but quickly notified the telephone company. Satterfield told him, the detective said, that the gadget only cost $42 to make, and they worked out a purchase price of $300.

"So he bought the box, a 4-by-6-inch device, which was encased in molded plastic so that it could not be repaired or dismantled without destroying it. He was unable to make the device operate, he continued, until he got written instructions from Satterfield and turned them with the gadget over to the telephone company experts.

"The next thing he heard, the private eye said, was a call from a shaken telephone official reporting: 'This damn thing works.'"

All of this caught Gerstein's attention, and he assigned his chief investigators to look into the matter. Posing as gamblers, investigators agreed to pay my father $1,000 for the boxes, and he made the mistake of returning to Miami from New York in March of 1961. When he gets there, they ask him to demonstrate the product to them. You know, "How does this thing work?" Sensing that things weren't right, he says, "The attachment of the device is simple, and you can follow the instructions yourself." My dad felt pretty sure that inventing something that could be used illegally was not a crime. He was not about to show them how to attach it to a Bell Telephone line.

In another article headlined, "Free Telephone Inventor Caught," it says: "Shaw told the investigator to go to a nearby dairy and call him from the pay phone. Arthur Huttoe, the assistant state attorney, said, 'The investigator did, using a dime which had been marked with nail polish. As soon as he finished talking and hung up, the dime was restored to him.'"

Gerstein twisted the law, and he claimed that my father's demonstration was the same as attaching the black box, and he proceeded to file charges and a warrant for Walter L. Shaw's arrest. My dad was arrested in March, but he jumped bail and returned to New York. That's when he was arrested in Oakland, New Jersey.

He beat the case in New York because of the Florida indictment, but he knew he'd be arrested if he came home to Florida. He decided to stay in Plainfield, New Jersey, for a while working with some investors on an answering service device. Then the subpoena for the hearings came around.

After being grilled by the McClellan Subcommittee, my dad was dismissed, and he was faced with a big dilemma. My sister, Linda, was getting married in Florida. Archie had told him that nothing could be done to help him if he returned to Florida and got himself arrested, but he wasn't going to miss his daughter's wedding, so he booked a flight home to Miami.

Just so he could be around his family for a few weeks, my dad rented a place behind our house to hide in after the wedding. He had explained to us that the police would be looking for him, and if he was found, he'd be going to jail. My father warned me never to mention his hideout. Like Archie had taught me, I was never going to open my mouth.

Nevertheless, two guys came to our door one day, and they're telling me that Archie sent them. Of course, if Archie sent them, they must be friends, and I took them behind our house to my dad's hiding place. Turns out they were with the Dade County Sheriff's Department, and my dad gets popped. Tricked by those two, I had talked, and my dad was cuffed and taken to jail. In spite of all Archie had taught me, I had opened my mouth like a fish.

I can remember telling my mother what had happened when she got home that day, and she called Grandpa Roberts with the details. Her father posted bond, and my dad came home, but seeing him handcuffed like that further fueled my hatred for the law.

It may have seemed a simple matter, but my dad's case got real complicated. My father put the money together to hire an attorney, the jury found him guilty of a misdemeanor, and his sentence would be levied by Circuit Judge Jack Falk. Since my father had no prior convictions, his attorney assured him that he'd get a suspended sentence. Meanwhile, though, the verdict was appealed.

I was going on fourteen by then, and my mom had me enrolled at North Miami Junior High School. That didn't last long. When I punched the vice principal, they threw me out. My poor mother had to come down and get me when I did that. I had cussed at a teacher and was sent to the vice principal's office. In those days, they could spank you with a paddle, and I told him I'd stick it up his ass if he tried to do that. He proceeded to try to paddle me, so I hit him, and they threw me out of school.

After being expelled from North Miami Junior High, I ended up taking special makeup classes to get into Miami Central. My dad's case had been in appeals court for a couple of years. As a matter of fact, he was actually in Hawaii doing a phone system for Jack Lord. Jack Lord played the role of Steve McGarrett in the television show called *Hawaii Five-O*, and my dad was doing some work for him over there.

I remember when my Mom called me into the kitchen one day. She says, "Dad's coming back. He lost his appeal, and they want him here for sentencing."

"What does that mean?" I asked her.

"Well, it means we're facing some hard times. We'll probably lose the house, for one," she tells me.

So my dad comes home. He was only expected to get probation if he'd cop out. If he would plead no contest, he was told he could take probation for the charges. That was the deal, but there was no fix in it for that. It would later come to light that he'd been set up. Because they were always in the courtroom, I know that Bell Telephone became part of the proceedings. Judge Falk held a private conference, and he told my father that his sentence would be lenient if he would divulge the inner workings of the black box. The attorneys, the judge, my father and a high ranking guy from Bell Laboratory were all there for that. My dad wouldn't do it. He wouldn't yield to their pressure, and they reconvened the sentence hearing. Instead of probation, he got a year and a day. I was in the courtroom when the judge told him that. The Bell executives were there, too.

My father did time on a misdemeanor, which is not on the books anymore. That was for Gerstein's bogus charge that he had attached the black box to a Bell Telephone line. He hadn't done that, but Gerstein made out like he did.

At the sentencing hearing, my dad's attorney argued that in the previous six months my dad had invented three new devices that would benefit the public. *The Miami News* quotes the attorney as saying: "Among these is a remarkable burglar alarm that literally lifts the phone and calls police when it is tripped by an intruder. Another device would make possible instant conference calls by governmental heads of state, without the present engineering complications. The man who has the know-how to do this should not be locked up." The following day, they ran the headline: "Phone-Cheat Genius Must Go to Jail."

Nobody goes away for misdemeanors—it's unheard of—but he got a year and a day in Dade County jail. That was strictly because he wouldn't cooperate. He wouldn't tell them how the black box worked, so he got the time. It had taken them six years to get him there, and they broke him financially during those years. It was 1965.

When my dad went to jail, he had told me to call Archie. I did what he told me, and I called him. "Uncle Archie?" I says. I needed to hear his voice.

"Don't ever call me on this line again," he told me.

I asked him, "Why?"

"Because it's probably being tapped, and I can't discuss this with you." Then he hung up on me. It wasn't about his phone line being tapped; he just wasn't helping us. Archie wasn't about to do anything for us. My dad had told me to call him for some money to help support our family, but Archie hangs up on me instead. I should have known the day I made that call that he wasn't our friend, but I was still a kid. I didn't want to know that then.

Many years later, I told my dad about that phone call. He said, "Thiel, they distance themselves from you when you go to jail. You're of no more value to them then, and that's your first hard lesson about this life you're choosing. They throw you away like damaged goods."

We lost everything when that sentence came down. It meant leaving Ives Estates and from then on we lived in places you wouldn't believe. Our whole lifestyle changed. At first, we moved into a two-bedroom shack at 95th Street and N.W. 2nd Avenue near Miami Central. I can't remember the thing, but I do remember being demoralized.

Grandpa Roberts had put up his house for my dad's bond in Florida, but there is a story behind that house. I already mentioned that my mom and dad bought a house for cash when they were married. After he left Southern Bell, though, we were making these treks across the country looking for opportunities for my dad's inventions. My mother says to him, "Listen, we're not going to sell the house, and it would be a nice gift for my mom and dad. They don't have a house. They'll probably never have one. Give it to them, and at least it stays in the family."

So my dad says, "Yeah, you're right, and we'll get something better when we hit that pot of gold." That's the kind of heart he had, and that's what he did—he gave it to them. And we could have been living there instead of moving around all the time. He should have kept the house and just let them live in it, but he had no sense about things like that.

When everything went down after his arrest, Grandma and Grandpa Roberts had figured out what he was doing, and I remember one of them saying to my mother, "We told you so." You know, "What did you expect from greasy, dirty-blooded Italians?" That came up in my father's face all the time. Just like Archie had told me, people hate Italians. My dad had given his in-laws a house, and they still called him a grease ball.

I was close to my mother's sister before she had children of her own. You could say I was her pet. We even lived with them for a time when my dad went to jail, and we had no other place to go. I remember my mother and my aunt yelling and arguing, and I heard my aunt say, "What do you expect from a jailbird?"

I walked into the kitchen, my aunt looked at me, and I said, "We'll never speak again. I'll sleep on the street before I'll ever sleep in this house again."

So that my mother didn't have to go to work, I got a job washing dishes and bussing tables at the International House of Pancakes. That only lasted so long. My mother wanted me back in school, and I wasn't going to fight her on that. At that point, I was still trying to do what she told me to do. I quit my job and went back to school, and that's when I decided to live with my nana. She was dying of cancer at the time.

My grandfather had already died, and Nana was living off 130-something Street. I can't remember the exact address. My mother was on 95th, so that wasn't very far away. Nana didn't have a car, and because I did, she wanted me to take her over to the Dade County jail to see my dad all the time. I took her over there on Saturdays and Sundays, but I would never go inside to see him. Not even for my nana would I go in there, but I used to take her to visit him, and I waited out in the parking lot.

I was mad as hell at my dad. You have to understand that I didn't know what had really happened to get him there. I felt betrayed as a kid, and once he was in jail, I couldn't hang on to the fact that he was innocent. You can imagine the kind of negative, nasty comments that were being whispered behind our backs. My dad was a known criminal, and I had to live all that down. Forty years later, it seems confusing that I turned on him, especially when you think about what I did to be called a criminal compared to what he did to be called a criminal. No comparison.

I guess I just didn't understand who those guys were and what they were doing—all the wise guys back in New York, I mean. I had been so taken with all of them at the McClellan Hearings. They meant a lot to me by telling me my dad wasn't a criminal. Carlo Gambino had told me my dad hadn't done anything wrong. "They're out to get your father," he had said. The people questioning my dad were the criminals, they just didn't get caught. The committee members, they had a license to steal. I thought we were the good guys.

So when he went to jail, I really turned on him. In my small, stupid mind, I was thinking that he should have been honest with me. When I confronted him about who they were—Archie, Joe Valachi, Sylvester, and them—he told me they were CPAs and jewelers. I know now that by telling me who they really were, he thought I'd go that way for sure. Early on, my mother and father knew where I was going. That must have killed them.

Even as a little child, I was rebellious and daring. I had that "damn you, devil-may-care, I can take it" attitude. I think my dad saw that. He saw an edge in me, and he thought it was better to lie about those guys. He figured that if I thought they got what they had doing the right thing, I might be influenced that way. I wasted a lot of years resenting him for that. All he was trying to do was protect me.

After everything happened, the investigations and all that, Ralph got off because his family had money. They bailed him out. My dad was the only one who went to jail. It must have been 1973 or 1974 when I saw Ralph again. He had lost an arm in an accident and had really aged since my knowing him as a kid. Ralph wasn't the handsome young guy I remembered, and it was sad to see him that way. He came into the house, and he says, "Oh, hi, Walter," like it was some kind of reunion or something.

My mom made one last-ditch effort for me during my dad's jail term. Because I was failing, she convinced me to take an English class in summer school to keep me from being held back again. I told her, "If I get held back again, I'm not finishing school. I don't want any more to do with it." I was seventeen years old by then. All my friends were older, and I was only in the tenth grade.

The genius and the flunky: my father quit school and ran away from home at sixteen; I met Connie at seventeen and did the same thing.

CHAPTER TWELVE

"I love him."
—Connie

It's 1965. My dad is in jail, and I'm starting to date a girl named Connie. She was in the accelerated class at Miami Central High School, and summer school was a way for her to prepare for senior year. Sixteen when I met her, Connie was the Key Club Sweetheart and Miss Miami Central. She was a beauty queen in my eyes, and I was a greaser in hers, just struggling to make it into high school. My persistence paid off, though, and after I followed her home one night, she agreed to start seeing me.

In the beginning, I told her my dad was away on business. Until I got to know her better, I didn't want to tell her the truth. Thinking back on it now, she probably knew anyway, but eventually I told her myself.

Connie and I were getting serious, and I told my mom I was going to marry her. She begged me not to do anything until my dad was out of jail. "Will you at least do that?" she pleaded with me. "Just wait until your dad comes home."

"Yeah, I'll do that," I told her.

So the day he was getting out of jail, my mom says, "I want you to stay home with your dad tonight."

I told her I didn't want to see him, and when he came in the front door, I got up to leave. He asks me, "Where are you going, Thiel?"

"I'm going out with my girlfriend," I told him.

"But I want you to stay home," he says.

"I'm not staying home. I'm going out with Connie, and I'm telling you right now that we're getting married," I said.

We got in a fight over that, and he slapped me. That was the first time in my life that my father had ever hit me. Being hot-

headed, there were words flying out of my mouth that I regret to
this day. I still remember my dad saying, "My God, what have I
done?" My mom followed that by telling me not to come back
until I could show my father some respect.

I headed for the door and said, "You can watch me leave now."

When I made it to Connie's house she knew right away that
something had happened. I told her my dad and I had argued. In
fact, I was so upset about some of the things that I'd said to him
that I put my fist through the windshield of my car. I had never
talked to my dad that way; and I hated myself for what I'd said to
him. He didn't deserve that from me.

The confrontation on the day he got out of jail was in August
1966, and all he wanted was to spend a little time with me. It was
no secret to him that I had been angry at him the whole time he
was away, never visiting him or anything. That first night home
was going to be his chance to tell me the truth about everything. I
was old enough to know by then.

Years later, he told me that had been his plan for that night.
He wanted to tell me why he went to jail, and that some very bad
choices had landed him there. That would have been my father's
chance at "truth day." Instead, I heard it all from Archie years later.
What a difference that might have made in my life, and I missed
it. "Truth day" had to come from a wise guy.

Anyway, a few days later my dad is all set to go chasing dollars in Oklahoma, and he made me promise not to get married
until his return. Shortly after that, Connie's mother found out we
had been sleeping together. She told my parents, and my dad made
the mistake of letting me know he was coming home. That's when
Connie and I decided to elope.

Some kids at school had told us that Folkston, Georgia,
allowed minors to get married without parental consent. Believing
that nonsense, we took a Greyhound bus to Georgia. When we got

there, a policeman noticed how young we were, and he notified Connie's parents that we were up there. Her mother told them to put us back on the bus and send us home. Surprisingly, she actually believed that we would be coming straight home, but my dad knew better. If the police had called him, he would have said, "Hold them there, I'm coming to get them."

Once again, I'm heading south on a Greyhound bus. Luckily, we had the cash to stay in a cheap hotel on Biscayne Boulevard back in Miami. I had gone to a friend of mine to ask for some money. Ten bucks a night that was costing us. Then I called my mother and said, "I'll come home when I know we can get married."

My mother says, "We'll agree to it, but please sit down and talk with us first. Don't do it like this."

"Okay, Mom," I tell her, "we'll do that."

When my dad gets back from Oklahoma, Connie and I sat with them for an hour or so at the Ranch House Restaurant on 7th Avenue. I wasn't expecting my dad to ask Connie whether we'd been sleeping together. In his quiet, naïve way, he asks, "Has my son been anything less than a gentleman with you? Has he been disrespectful to you?"

Connie didn't know what he meant, so she says, "No; he loves me, and I love him."

"I don't mean it like that, Connie. Has he slept with you?" my dad asked her.

She looked at me, and her non-answer was the answer. My father stood up and left the table. I'll never forget it, my mother said, "You put the dagger in his heart, Thiel. You finally got to hurt him. God help you this time."

When we went to Connie's, her parents had put all her belongings on their front doorstep. It should be no surprise that they never wanted her to marry me. They saw the way I was doing things. They knew where I was going with their daughter.

Knowing they couldn't stop it, both sides agreed to our marriage, and Connie and I were married in the Church of the Nazarene on 95th Street and 7th Avenue on March 12, 1967. Except for Connie's mother, everyone attended the wedding. Her dad was there, but her mother refused to come. Connie's mom hated me at first, but she came around. This is down the road—a lot of water under the bridge—but when Connie later remarried, which tells you we were eventually divorced, her mother says to me one day, "You're the only son-in-law I ever had." She came to my side eventually.

Connie and I left for Oklahoma the night we were married. My dad hadn't finished his business there, talking to some investors about one of his inventions. At that point, he was working on the conference call. Why did we go with my dad to Oklahoma? Where was I going to go with a young wife at nineteen? Connie was barely seventeen, and we had no money and no education. He didn't want us on the streets of Miami, so he says, "You're coming with me to Oklahoma, and we'll try to make it there. You're not staying here by yourselves." My mom went everywhere with my dad. Linda was gone, but my little sister, Crystal, came along with us, too.

As usual, the guys in Oklahoma turned out to be full of crap. They wanted to invest in an answering service, which isn't what my dad had in mind, so we drove from there to Findlay, Ohio. My father always had two or three guys on the line, and Ohio was his backup after Oklahoma failed. Like I said, my dad was always chasing dollars. In Findlay, he had a backer by the name of Dr. Razor, an obstetrician who started Buckeye Communications with him. Razor and my dad got a tower for mobile units and pagers, but he was still working on the conference call.

It wasn't too long after getting there that Connie was suffering from morning sickness. Dr. Razor examined her and told us she was pregnant. On November 18, 1967, our baby girl, Michele Marie, was born. We'd all been living in a tri-level house in Findlay. The business was on the first floor, my parents' and Crystal's bedrooms were on the second floor, and the third floor was for Connie and me.

I was working at a clothing store in downtown Findlay on Main Street. My dad had said, "With the money you bank, you can buy a car." Everything I earned went to that end, and the first car I bought was a 1968 Chevy Camaro, all souped up. I paid cash for that car, and it gave me some independence.

It was no secret that I hated Findlay, Ohio, and I wanted to go home to Miami soon after we got there. So my dad says, "Well, I'll drive my car, and we'll go there for Christmas week to introduce the baby to Connie's parents." We did that, which endeared me some to them. In my favor, I was all for having a family relationship with my new in-laws.

That trip home to Miami was all it took for me. After Christmas, I decided to go back to Ohio to get our stuff; Connie and I were moving back to Florida. "You think you can do that on your own?" my dad asked us.

"Yeah, I can do it. I'm ready to go," I answered. Turns out, my dad ended up coming home, too. He had struck a deal with two investors on the conference call, and we all headed back to Miami. His backers and him formed a company to market and sell the conference calling equipment, and by early 1968, my father was earning a good salary plus the money he was making from royalties and stock.

As for me, when we made it home, I was working at Schiff's Shoe Store making minimum wage and a small commission. My dad was giving us a hundred bucks a week just so we could make it. He had promised to help us if I'd pass my GED (General Equivalency Diploma) test to graduate from high school and go on to enroll at Dade Junior College. Connie had to go to work to make ends meet, and before long, she was pregnant again. Things were real tough on us financially.

Trying to make a little more money, I went to work selling cars for a place called Bell Ford. That's when the fast dollar started for me. I met some shady guys there. James Bell, an Indian, robbed a bunch of money orders and had me cash them and pass them. That netted me $5,000, and also my second arrest. The first had been during our brief trip back to Miami from Findlay, Ohio, at Christmastime. My buddy and I shoplifted two pairs of swim trunks and were arrested in the parking lot. My first incarceration lasted only a few hours.

The second time around, I was placed on probation for three years and ordered to repay the $5,000. The judge warned me, though, that if I ever appeared before her again, she would not be so lenient.

I was getting tired of the way we were struggling. I'd spent too many years watching my parents trying to make it before me. By then, I had experienced both poverty and living comfortably, and I was seeing the legitimate road to living well as taking too long. Going to school and working wasn't cutting it for me, and there was only one way to make money fast as far as I knew. It would be risky, but I wasn't afraid of that. I wasn't gonna do poverty with my own family. We had our little girl, and my son, Randolph Lewis Shaw, had come along on July 12, 1969.

So my dad and I are both back in Florida at this point. For the first time, he was feeling secure that there was a lot of money to be made with his newest invention, and there was, but he never saw any of it. Even with a patent on it, he got nothing after a few months of being in business with his new partners, and I'll get to the reason behind that. In my mind, it was time to call Uncle Archie. I didn't see myself as having a choice. I was ready to go down the wrong road, and I was looking forward to it.

With my dog *Shep* about the time
I was getting started in the rackets, 1968.

CHAPTER THIRTEEN

"The patent system added the fuel of interest
to the fire of genius."
—Abraham Lincoln

Most people don't understand what it means to have a
patent on something. With anything you patent, you
should be getting royalties from those who use it, but it doesn't
always work out that way. We found that out from Attorney F. Lee
Bailey.

Prior to his disbarment, Bailey served as a criminal defense
attorney. He's had his defeats and personal troubles with the law,
but Lee is also famous for his big wins. Despite his difficulties, he
has a reputation for being one of the best defense lawyers in
American legal history. He was the one who taught my dad and
me that a patent is only as good as the money you have to defend it.

First off, if you make a patent and somebody infringes, you
need to have been making the maintenance fees every year; sec-
ondly, you have to be willing to go to court to defend your patent;
and thirdly, back when we consulted with him, when you filed suit
you had to put up three times the amount of the lawsuit in a court
registry. And that's on a case you might lose in the end.

Let's say you're suing somebody for $100,000 for using your
invention. You have to put up $300,000 in the court registry to
begin litigation. So my dad was trapped again. He never had the
money to keep up with the maintenance fees, and his patents
would expire. And even if he had been able to pay the fees, he
never had the money to put up in a court registry, which meant all
of his prototypes were stolen by big corporations and wealthy
businessmen. As a matter of fact, without mentioning any names
here, that just happened again. One of the biggest companies in

the world just ran with another one of his ideas, his very last patented invention, having to do with voice recognition.

F. Lee Bailey could have defended my father. We were talking to him about all of my dad's inventions at that point. When we went to see him, he says, "You have a case, and you will probably win, but it will take several years. And the trouble is you have to put up the fees for it in case you lose." He went on to say, "Walter, give me $50,000, and I'll defend it, but I have to be retained." Unfortunately, Bailey wouldn't take it on a contingency basis, but he thought we would have won. He couldn't be sure, but he didn't seem to have any doubt.

When that happened, I wasn't making that kind of money yet. I was doing some bad stuff, but I wasn't making big money. If memory serves, it was 1969, and I was just getting into jewel thieving. Because he'd stood up for them in the McClellan Hearings, you might wonder why the wise guys wouldn't put up some money for my dad. They didn't care. They weren't earning off him anymore. They loved him, but they couldn't earn off him because he wouldn't be part of them.

Time and time again, he'd been told, "Sue us. You want to stop us; sue us." American businessmen blatantly screwed Walter L. Shaw out of the three biggest inventions of his life: the speakerphone, the conference call and call forwarding. And you'll remember a remote apparatus being invented for the bookmakers. He went even further than that with "Extend-a-Watts."

Prior to my dad's invention of that one, you could only dial long distance calls with watts lines. A watts line is a special "800" type number with a fee for unlimited calls, or you could pick a plan for a specific number of calls. Also, you could only use a watts phone line from your office or wherever it was located. My dad made "Extend-a-Watts," where you could gain access to the line any place in the world and go out over it by remote. If you had a

watts line in your office and it was after hours and you were at
home and you didn't want to go back to your office, with "Extend-
a-Watts" you could call into your office, hit a tone, and dial out just
like you were in your office. He was a real genius with electronics.

When my dad invented the conference call, two investors out
of Chicago, who shall remain nameless, came to Florida and made
a deal with him. They formed a corporation together, and they
called it Com-u-trol Communications. My dad was being paid
$350 a week; and he would get a 25 percent royalty on every unit
sold. They sold distributorships, (the one in Florida was sold for
$250,000 up front), and every distributorship had to buy at least
500 units a month to keep their distributorship alive. Given the
deal they had struck, just off the conference call alone, my dad
would have been a multi-millionaire.

Those two guys from Chicago were very shrewd, great mar-
keting guys. As the story goes, they got a call from a company in
Los Angeles. The two of them went out there, and the executives
of that company said, "Look, we'd like to merge with you." Well,
the patent agreement was made with Com-u-trol, and if you bank-
rupt Com-u-trol, it's over. The patent agreement was not transferable.

My father owned a third of the company, but those guys
thought, *Merge, go public, grab the IPO, and tell the inventor "good-
bye."* When that happened, they cut off my dad's paycheck, he lost
his house, and my parents' cars were repossessed. That was 1971,
and my mom and dad were without anything again. His stock was
valueless, the assets were transferred to the merger, and any debt
remained. The year they went with the company in California, the
conference call alone did $152,000,000 worldwide. No doubt, they
robbed my dad.

People need to understand that it wasn't any "Puff the Magic
Dragon" when my dad sat down and put pen to paper on his
inventions. It didn't happen like that. My dad was making his

little drawings on the conference call for fourteen years before it came to fruition. Sketch after sketch after sketch, and that's why he was entitled to get paid for it.

Extend-a-Watts didn't just happen, either. The conference call and Extend-a-Watts were years in the making with that poor man. He was testing and retesting. My dad was buying parts and making models at the kitchen table, just living for the moment he could put one of them in one of his little plastic boxes and make a demonstration. I was there for that. It didn't happen overnight for my father.

Ironically, though, the only invention my dad is known for is the black box, but that one made him infamous, not famous. It defeated the direct dialing system. Before direct dialing, you had to place a call through an operator. The only way the black box could work was with direct dialing. That's why he says, "You got a choice: You want to stop me, get rid of the direct dialing system. Otherwise, this lives." That's what he told them behind closed doors before his sentencing hearing in 1965. The Bell guys were there for that.

He even went a step further in the 1970s by bouncing it off satellites in the sky. That was done for Meyer Lansky. When Lansky faced tax evasion charges in the 1970s, he fled to Israel, where he lived for two years before being deported to the United States. While Lansky was fighting for his freedom from over there, my dad made a box for him. Using the satellites allowed Lansky to make toll-free, untraceable calls to America. As it turned out, Lansky was acquitted in 1974.

It is also ironic that the black box, the only invention my dad was really ever credited for, wasn't patented. However, it didn't need to be. Like I said, no one ever figured it out. I went to the Miami papers and got every article I could find about my father. A reporter for the *Miami News* headlined an article: "Tiny Black

Box that Frightens a Giant." That article was about the black box that couldn't be broken. Nobody could figure out how it worked, and Bell hated him for that. The reporter says in that one, "Widespread sale of the gadget might even cause junking of the nationwide, billion-dollar direct dialing system."

If my dad hadn't been the good guy that he was, they never would have stopped him. He knew the system too well. There weren't any limits with that thing. He could manage toll-free access to anywhere in the world. What he could do with the phone lines was like a virus in a computer system. That's why Bell was so upset about it. It was a parasite on their system. The black box technology was the glitch. Bell, one of the biggest companies in the world, couldn't figure it out. I'm still amazed when I think that *my dad* made those things. He could make them individually, and he could make six in a day.

Tiny Black Box That Frightens A Giant

By VERNE O. WILLIAMS
Reporter of The Miami News

A tiny black box that threatens to "steal" millions of dollars from the telephone company has brought on a kingsize legal battle here.

I also have an article that says, "Walter Shaw is called 'Edison of the underworld.'" In my view, that is a great honor. I don't care if they used the word "underworld." The point is they recognized him in that league. What I do care about, however, is that every other thing he ever did was thrown out. They just keep going back to the black box. The speakerphone was developed for polio victims; the alert system in Alaska was installed for our national security, and the hot line between Washington and Moscow, sometimes called the "red phone," which my father helped to establish in August 1963, was devised as a direct result of the Cuban Missile Crisis. Call forwarding, conference calling, voice recognition—they were all created after the black box. His best work was ahead of him when he came up with that for the mob!

It should come as no surprise that my father hasn't been inducted into the Inventors Hall of Fame in Akron, Ohio. So far, he's been rejected, and I know it's because of his criminal past. They haven't turned me down completely, but they've put me off. I think it will get done eventually, but I probably won't see it in my lifetime. I keep submitting him every year, and I recently asked the lady on the phone, "Do you think he'll ever be selected?"

She says, "I think one day, Walter, they'll accept him."

The black box can be seen as a device for ill gain, but what about his thirty-nine patented inventions? They always go back to that one. Every article written about my dad concerns the black box. When I think about it, though, every article written about me mentions my dad and the black box. I suppose I've wanted it that way. I'm proud of my dad. Even for him and me, though, it all comes down to the existence of a black box, the "parasite" they called it at the hearings. I'm not in the same playing field as my dad, but everything I became was because of him. Even the wise guys would say, "Oh, the young kid, young Shaw, the inventor's son." The only reason I got in the door was because of my dad. I'd have never gotten in on my own.

When my father lost his stock in Com-u-trol, he and my mother were destitute again. By then, I had met a kid named Jimmy Miller at a college party, and he introduced me to his step-father, Carl Miller, a known extortionist. Carl knew about the black boxes, and I offered to supply him with those for $5,000 up front and $1,500 a unit. That would get me the money I needed to pay off the $5,000 I owed for passing those stolen money orders, and it would take care of my parents. Equally desperate, my dad was willing to make the boxes again. Carl agreed to the unit cost of the boxes, but he turned me down on the front money. Payment would only be made upon delivery. More on this later, but that's how I met Frank Sacco, probably the most brutal extortionist of any of them.

In any event, without the black box, I wouldn't have met Archie; I'd never have met Frank Sacco and Carl Miller, and I never would have been claimed by Anthony. If it wasn't for the black box, I'd never have met Pete Salerno or joined the Dinner Set Gang. I would never have met any of those guys if it wasn't for the black box.

I'll say it again: there are two stories here, but they are inter-twined. The difference is, my father could have had his story with-out me, but I never would have had mine. What I'm getting at here is the black box again. If my dad hadn't invented that, his story would have been different. Even more dramatically, though, what follows isn't the way I'd be telling the rest of my story. The black box was the beginning of the wrong road for me. Even after I got in, it allowed my deeper penetration into the underworld.

You might say that it was the worst thing that ever happened to either of us, and that is probably true. I am quick to say that my life has been wasted, but I have never blamed my father for that. You know, I've never resented him for hooking up with those guys. Oh, yeah, I was mad at him for not telling me the truth when

I was a kid, but that didn't last. My dad was probably the kindest, gentlest soul I have ever met in my life. How could I resent that? He wasn't a guy who could hurt anybody. My dad wouldn't go that far. He wouldn't cross that line. He was a good guy among the wise guys, and that's what they loved about him.

It was amazing to me that, even when people robbed him, kicked him, and failed to recognize him for what he was inventing, he always thought the sun would come out again. My father always saw the glass as half full. He never knew how to quit, and that may be the one good gene I got from him. I have tenacity, too, but most of the time I was using that good gene in a bad way—the mutant. Same gene, different use for it: If he could draw it, he could make it. If I could get close to it, I could steal it. It took my dad years and years to make something happen. Down the road, it took me one night. Everyone who robbed my dad had a license to steal, but just like Carlo Gambino told me, I didn't need one.

Malloy &
Malloy, P.A.

"Since 1969"
Registered Patent Attorneys
Trial and Appellate Counsel
Internet: malloylaw.com

Patent, Trademark & Copyright Law

Miami Office
2800 S.W. Third Avenue
Miami, Florida 33129
Telephone (305) 858-8000
Facsimile (305) 858-0008

Ft. Lauderdale Office
2101 West Commercial Blvd.
Reply to: Miami Office
Broward (954) 525-9611
Florida (800) 337-7239

March 28, 2003

Walter Shaw, Jr.

    Re: General Patent Matter
        In the name of: Walter H. L. Shaw
        Our Ref.: 7.216.00

TO WHOM IT MAY CONCERN:

    After checking certain records of the U.S. Patent and Trademark Office, we note that Walter Shaw, Sr. was awarded several U.S. patents for various inventions relating to telephone / communication systems, such as (but not necessarily limited to):

U.S. Pat. No.	Issued	Title:
2,575,844	Nov. 20, 1951	FEEDBACK NEUTRALIZATION MEANS FOR TELEPHONE SYSTEMS
2,844,659	July 22, 1958	TWO-WAY COMMUNICATION UNIT
3,389,224	June 18, 1968	CONFERENCE CONNECTION & CONTROL DEVICE FOR TELEPHONE SUBSCRIBER LINES
3,406,261	Oct. 15, 1968	TELEPHONE SWITCHBOARD CALL TRANSFER DEVICE
3,553,373	Jan. 5, 1971	MANUAL REROUTER SYSTEM FOR TELEPHONE SUBSCRIBER STATION WITH COMBINED CONFERENCE CALL FEATURE
3,591,727	July 6, 1971	AUTOMATIC REROUTING SYSTEM FOR TELEPHONE SUBSCRIBER STATION
3,610,827	October 5, 1971	CONFERENCE CALL EQUIPMENT

Also, these records indicate that Walter Shaw engaged the services of my grandfather, John Cyril Malloy, an attorney who helped establish this law firm in Miami.

    By the way, I am a registered patent attorney and would be glad to answer any questions you might have regarding these matters or any other patent issues.

March 28, 2003
Page 2

    Kindest regards,

                      Very truly yours,

                      Jennie S. Malloy
                      For the Firm

A letter submitted to the National Inventors Hall of Fame.

PART TWO

REBELLION

PREFACE TO PART TWO

"Ask me no questions, and I'll tell you no lies."
—Walter T. Shaw

Before I chose my profession in the organization, jewel thieving, my criminal activities were multifaceted. I was trying on a lot of things in the rackets. I'd extort, write bad checks, make counterfeit money, forge, rob—I could do it all. That was my goal. There was never going to be a Christmas in my house without a tree and lots of gifts. I just wasn't going to live my life that way.

The fact that my father and I were estranged almost from the time we came home from Findlay, Ohio, in 1968, until 1995 should tell you something. It isn't that I didn't see him from time to time. I did. But it was killing him to see what I was doing with my life. He hadn't been willing to cross the line; my dad wouldn't go any further than the boxes. I was willing to do anything. He was a good guy, and I wanted to be a wise guy. He knew that.

So I didn't come around my parents' house very often. My mom's knowing that I had been accused of being connected with certain guys disappearing and other atrocities—I couldn't deal with the hurt in her eyes. How could any mother stand that? She cried every time she saw me, asking, "Thiel, are those things true that we're hearing and reading about you?"

And I always said, "Ask me no questions, and I'll tell you no lies." I'm not going to tell her a lie just to make her feel better. When I was most involved with the "Dinnertime Burglars," the infrequency of my visits with my parents didn't change. I avoided both of them until I got to prison. The choice was no longer mine while I was locked up.

When I first went in, my mother wasn't going to stop coming, but my father came just one time. That's when he delivered my boss's message that I should die a soldier's death. It disturbed him so much to see me locked up that he never returned. My mother says to me, "Dad can't do this as well as I can, Thiel, but you're my son. I don't care if they put you on death row, you're still my son." As it turned out, they did put me on death row, but I'm getting ahead of my story.

It is accurate to say that my father was like a shadowy presence during the years we were estranged. Turns out we were both in prison for part of that time. Out of desperation, my dad made some more bad choices, but true to his nature, he never went past the black boxes. Despite his own mistakes, he tried hard to keep me straight, but that was never going to happen. He knew that early on, probably from the day I started wearing my little black trench coat with Uncle Archie.

The first time I got a look at something different in life was meeting Archie, and the first time I was set apart was at Oakland Military Academy. When that headline came out saying that my dad was a criminal, I was suddenly separated from the other boys. Even though I'm thinking he's innocent, I went from being just a kid to being labeled a gangster's kid, and that was the beginning of something bad.

My mother always said that was the turning point in my life. She had noticed a total personality change in me when I got off that Greyhound bus in Miami. She says, "You turned. You twisted, Thiel."

I'm sure my father felt responsible for turning me. That must have been his private hell, his secret prison to know that all the things he was reading about and hearing about me were true. My mother kept asking, but he knew they were true. Short of death or going to prison, though, nothing was going to change my direction. My parents might have remembered me as a little kid with big brown eyes, but they lost control early on.

Society could write what they wanted to write about Walter L. Shaw. He was called a gangster because he was associated with "known" thugs, but he was never a wise guy. They threw him in the pot with them, regardless. I hated that.

By that action of this society we live in, I put a bat in my hand. I realized I had to go through life defending myself for being the son of a gangster. I had to live up to that label, good or bad. And all those years, my father was still trying to make it with his inventions, always working on something to make the next demonstration.

My father was paid for something he made. I was looking to get made. He was giving, and I was taking. Either way, the story is tragic.

CHAPTER FOURTEEN

"He's nineteen, and he thinks he's the godfather."
—Carl Miller, Extortionist

Back when I was pressured to raise $5,000 to make good on the stolen money orders, Carl Miller had seen my desperation. When he wouldn't pay up front for the boxes my dad was making for him, he offered me a job to earn some good money. His business, Standard Plastering Company, was just a front for his criminal activities. Carl was deeply entrenched in South Florida's Mafia organization, and he referred me to a higher up, Frank Sacco.

A ruthless extortionist, Sacco had his headquarters in New York, but his criminal activities extended as far south as Miami. He hired me as a courier, and it was my job to carry a briefcase from Miami International Airport to New York's La Guardia via JFK. I would stash the case in a locker at La Guardia, and hand off the key to one of Sacco's henchmen in a pre-arranged location. In exchange for the key to the locker, he gave me $500. I was doing that three times a week, and $1,500 was a lot of money to me. It didn't take too long for me to move my wife and two kids into the Gulf Air Apartments, luxurious accommodations to my way of thinking. But I was looking for even more.

Frank Sacco had one rule: never open the case. Under no circumstances was I supposed to open a case. I had delivered a lot of cases before I opened the first one. It was seven, eight, nine months before I looked inside. Never, not once had it crossed my mind to open one. I just took a shot one day. I'm sitting in an enclosed stall with the case, and I decide to pry it open.

It took me what seemed like a long time to count it—extortion money, loan shark money—high interest. Money on the streets could be had at 12 percent interest a week. That means a loan for a $1,000 would cost you $1,254 in two weeks. I had no idea how much was in that attaché case. All wrapped up in rubber bands it turned out to be $96,000. *If I decide to take this*, I'm thinking, *how am I going to hide it?*

So I get to JFK on Long Island that day, and I put the case in a locker there before catching a cab to La Guardia. When I get to La Guardia, I stage a phony beating by punching myself and all that nonsense in the men's room. When I come out of the stall, one of the pick-up men says, "What happened, kid?"

"I don't know," I tell him. "Some guys were waiting for me that I never seen before."

"Oh, some guys just mysteriously appeared?" one of them started to stick me.

"Hear him out," says the other one.

And I answered, "Yeah, they blind-sided me, asked me for the case, and I gave it to them before I got it into the locker."

"Okay, kid, here's your envelope. Go on back to Florida. We'll talk to Carl about it." They knew exactly how to handle that situation: Act like you believe it, give him the money anyway, and see you later. So I got on a plane and went back to Florida.

Maybe a week or two later on a car lot, I see a chocolate brown Cadillac coupe and a yellow El Dorado with a black top. I told the guy, "I'll take both of them." I gave the yellow one to my dad. He believed me when I told him I had "borrowed" the money from Carl Miller. In fact, I gave it to him at a restaurant. We went to Carino's that night, and I surprised him and my mother. I was wearing a new suit, top of the line in those days, a Petrocelli from Peter Kent. They don't even make them anymore, but it was five hundred, which was a lot of money for a suit back then.

I was nineteen at the time, and I went out to the racetrack a few days later. I'll never forget it. Two guys, two of Sacco's henchmen, walked up to me and said, "What are you doing here?"

"I'm gambling, like you."

"You're gambling like us, huh?" I'm asking for $500 a trip, and two months later I'm gambling like them? Except to go there to find Archie on occasion, I'd never been near a racetrack before.

"Yeah," I tell him. They were notching the notes at that point. Notching the notes means "he just bought a Cadillac." They were putting it together. Two months before that, I was destitute. Then all of a sudden I'm buying a coupe for me and an El Dorado for my father. They're figuring it all out. The wise guys give you time to hang yourself. They weren't going to accuse me until they knew, and I gave them the ammunition by flaunting how I was living.

Months had gone by. They gave me all the rope I needed. I should have known something was up; I hadn't gotten a trip for a while. I didn't suspect anything, though. Young and stupid, I actually thought I was getting away with it! Buying those cars and all the rest of it. Totally ridiculous when I think about it now. It was a child's mind thinking that way. Would I do it differently? Yeah, but I wasn't them yet.

So Carl calls me up, and he says, "Walt, come on over to the warehouse. I've got a job for you."

"Great," I tell him. I was ecstatic to get back at it again. So I shaved and got dressed, and I made sure to take the .38 special with me. Those days, you could even take a gun with you on the plane. I was doing my normal routine, and I stashed the gun in the boot of the Corvette. I had bought my wife a Corvette, too, white with black interior. Stupid.

When I get to Carl's warehouse on the north side of Miami, I see his car and a couple of others. At the time, I didn't think anything of it. It isn't that it was unusual to have more than Carl there, but it was late in the day, which was unusual. Carl had said, "Come in the afternoon," which, looking back on it now meant that the employees at Standard Plastering would be done for the day.

So I drive up, park the car and get out. Because I knew I was just picking up my airline tickets, I didn't bring the gun in with me. I just walked up to the building, and all of a sudden, the door opens and two guys step out. One was circling around me, and then he went over by my Corvette.

I says, "Wait a minute, guys, I've got to go back to my car."

"If you ain't got it on you, kid, you're not getting it," he says. Then I knew. They knew what I was going back for.

Now Carl comes out, and he says, "Walter, what a beautiful Corvette. Am I right that you also bought a Coupe DeVille? My guys tell me that you've been out to the tracks lately, too. You look good, kid, you look good. I just gotta know, though. Where did you get the money? If I didn't know better, I might think your good father died and left you $96,000. Walter, how in the world did you ever think you'd get away with this?"

"Get away with what?"

"Please," he says, "I'm almost sixty. I've lived a few lifetimes, and you're just starting out. How did you think you could rob me and get away with it? Don't play games with me, Walter."

I knew I was caught then, but I thought he would just ask me to give him the money back. I said, "Well, Carl..."

"No, there's no 'well, Carl' about it."

One of the men steps in front. BOOM! The lights went out! Then I got hit on the side where the other one was standing. Boom! Boom! Boom! I mean, even though it was over in three or four minutes, it was brutal, and I was out for over an hour after that.

When I found myself lying face up in the blinding sun, I had never been so upset. I'm bleeding out of the mouth, sand is sticking to my face and my sides felt mutilated. That's when I decided to go out to the car for the snub nose, and I crawled my way back into the warehouse. It was just him and me then. The other two had left. Carl was sitting there alone, and I shoved the gun in his face.

He says, "You're going to shoot me? You robbed me, and you're going to shoot me? Now, how much sense does that make?"

I said, "Carl, I'm going to tell you something. Put this on the books. Tell the street that if anybody ever comes to me again, right, wrong or indifferent, and gives me a beating like this, kill me, because I will kill them the next time."

"You think you will, huh?"

"I know I will," I say to him. "And do you know why I'm not going to shoot you this time?"

"No, tell me why," he says to me.

I tell him, "Because I know I did wrong. I bit the hand that feeds me."

And he says to me, "You are saying that right, but you know what? You're finished with us. You've just cut your earning off, and you got a month to come up with the $96,000. Frank will be down to straighten it out with you, and you better come up with it. But I helped you, and you're going to shoot me? You're crazy, kid."

He knew I wouldn't shoot him. I didn't have the edge in my favor to do it. Even though I got beat up pretty good, I knew I didn't have the edge in my favor. *I'm going to shoot the guy I robbed?* That may happen in a stickup, but not where I was coming from. I'm going to shoot the guy I robbed? What kind of logic is that? I had worked for Carl for about a year when that happened.

Carl laid me on the couch after I confronted him. His wife appeared from somewhere and put a steak on my face. He had really saved me that afternoon. They were going to break my face, put me away, and he stopped them. I remember that. I was already on the ground and real messed up, but he held them off. I asked, "Carl, why didn't you let them finish it?"

"Because," he tells me, "I thought you'd had enough. If they had done that, you wouldn't have been repairable." He told me again, though, that they would kill me if I didn't come up with the money. "You broke the rules, kid, and out of respect for your dad, we didn't kill you, but you gotta come up with the $96,000."

I do think they would have killed me if it weren't for my dad. They loved my father, and I know that had a lot to do with it. But they also knew I would have stolen from them again.

The day after I got that beating, I had to be at my sister Linda's wedding. I'm there wearing sunglasses with my whole face caved in. Broken ribs. I was in bad shape. Because I had stumbled home the previous night and gone straight to bed, I didn't know how bad it was. I was just trying to sleep it off.

My dad was livid when he saw me. He knew I was probably guilty—had broken the rules—but he also knew that Carl knew better than to beat me before calling for a sit-down. A sit-down is a meeting between the family leaders to settle disputes. The unbelievable part of this story is that my dad is the one who called for the sit-down after the beating.

When we sat down with Carl at Lum's Restaurant in Opa-locka, I remember listening to my father, and I'm thinking, "*Who is this man?*" My father is sitting there challenging *them*. I'll never forget it. He looked at me, stood up and he says, "If you hit him again, then we have a problem." That's how he talked. And he says, "But you're paid in full now because you chose to hit him first."

"Dad, where did that come from?" I remember asking him.

He said, "I know the rules, Thiel, I know the rules."

I was shocked by what my dad was doing that day. I always believed that he wasn't one of them, but he knew how it worked. He knew the rules. Rules are: You try a guy first at a sit-down. In my dad's eyes, deciding to beat me before a sit-down was a serious breach of Mafia etiquette. "Sacco got paid when you beat Walter!" he screamed at Carl.

After all this went down, Carl said, "The kid's crazy. He's got no fear, no sense of up and down. He's nineteen, and he thinks he's the godfather." That's about the time that a wise guy named Anthony, who was on the up and rise, started hearing stories about me when he was down in Miami. When I met up with him, he had already heard that I was fearless. The word had traveled the gamut. That's what you want: You want to know that there is no reverse in this guy's life. There's no backing up—no getting out, in other words.

But my dad once said to me, "They respect you because they fear you, Thiel, and that is a false respect. That isn't a compliment, to be respected out of fear." The way to achieve respect is the way he did it. My dad distanced himself from them because he knew he wasn't like them. When you're in that world, you think it's all right to cheat, to have affairs, to do whatever, and my dad was not in that world. They knew he was too kind for any of that. They respected him for his mind; he was like Meyer Lansky, a real genius in the mob. Walter Shaw, Sr. was admired by them because he was brilliant, a nice guy, and they respected that. He was his own man. Once he got his jail time behind him, he wanted to move on. It was out of desperation that he slipped again later on.

Anyway, there was huge fallout after the sit-down. This is where it got serious, and also where I get saved again. A guy comes down to see Carl, and they call my dad and me to Coney Island, a place on Collins Avenue in North Miami. I called the guy Vinny Sunglasses—he wore these mirrored sunglasses all the time.

My dad goes through his spiel again, and Vinny says, "Listen, I know what you're saying, and I respect that Mr. Shaw." He's looking at my dad. "But you know what? I don't care. He's not walking. We want the money. You can go to whoever you think you can go to, but I'm telling you, I want the money, or I'm putting your son in Biscayne Bay. That's the deal. I don't care who you run to."

For the next month, I keep a gun on me constantly. I sleep with it, I don't go anywhere without it. But nothing happens. Soon after that, Frank Sacco, Carl Miller, and Harry Freedman were indicted, and the word on the street had it that I was being subpoenaed to testify against them. Fearing what might happen because of that, I was hiding out with my wife and kids in Hollywood, Florida. Turns out Miller's guys find me, and Carl's message was clear: "Don't show yourself until the trial is over."

All three of them made bond, and I was warned to keep hiding out if I wanted to stay alive. Carl came to see me, and he warned me again, "They're looking for you to testify."

"I'm not talking," I told him.

"Frank is nervous," he says. "You're twenty years old, and he wants to eliminate all the branches."

"Okay, you've warned me." Connie, our two kids and I went to Ocala then, and I stayed there until it was all over. I didn't understand why at the time, but Carl also told me the $96,000 was history.

Turns out, Carl was flipping and testifying for the government, which puts Frank away and everybody else involved. When the trial ended, Frank Sacco got fifty-five years and Miller was sentenced to twelve months at Eglin Air Force Base. I came out of hiding up in Ocala and moved my family back to Miami.

With the courier job dried up, I was looking for cash flow opportunities. That's when I made a move and took a truckload of paintings to the flea market. I had done a dirty deal in lifting those paintings from a guy in Georgia, but I put a booth together and was selling them. Running a booth at the flea market wasn't my thing. Connie ran the booth, and I sat there and played cards with the guy who ran the place. I'm getting ahead of my story here. I had also started robbing people with the Dinner Set Gang by 1969, but it's important to include here how my life was saved after stealing the $96,000.

As the story goes, I'm playing canasta with this guy, and he's telling me about a friend of his, Vinny. "Vinny's the guy I'm with," he says.

I says, "Vinny? I call him Vinny Sunglasses. Is that the same guy?"

"Yeah, he always wears those mirrored sunglasses, right?"

"Yeah," I answered.

"Well, he opened a bar up in Miramar," he tells me.

"He did, huh?

"Yeah, he's putting a nightclub together," he tells me. "He's one of my dearest friends, and he got killed the other day."

"He got killed?" I asked him, shocked.

"Yeah, a guy shot him. He was over there doing his thing, just hanging out, and he got into it with one of the tradesmen, a carpenter. They got into an argument, and the guy pulled a .22 on him. Vinny says, 'If you don't use it, I'm going to stick it up your ass.' Knowing who he was, the guy was so terrified he unloaded on him, dropped him."

I jumped up and ran around the office. "No, shit!" I said, "That's fantastic!"

The guy's looking at me, and he says, "What do you mean, fantastic?! He's a friend of mine. What are you, nuts?!" Then I tell him the whole story.

I remember him saying, "You're lucky, because he didn't care about all that. He was a real renegade. He would have killed you, kid. He didn't care about the rules."

I find out years later that this guy was up in rank. They loved him. Vinny was a huge earner, which means he made a lot of money for the rackets, and he sat right next to a boss. In other words, he only answered to one guy, and that was the boss. He didn't have anybody underneath him, a co-captain or a captain, a regional or district boss. He answered only to a boss, like a Genovese or a Gambino. Because he had enough juice, he didn't have to answer to anybody else.

What I'm saying is, if it came down the road, he would give them the $96,000 out of his own pocket for whacking me. It was a principle thing with him. I had broken protocol, and I thought I got away with it. Vinny wasn't going to let that happen, and Carl brought him in because of that. They also happened to be good friends. When I heard that Vinny got whacked, I understood why Miller had told me that the $96,000 was history. The hit man was dead.

About the time I was getting in too deep, my father was getting back into it, too. In addition to Carl, he found someone else interested in the boxes, and he told me the guy was a dominant force on the way up. He was in touch with Anthony, and I remember the day he told me that. This is one of the times he slipped. He'd been screwed on the conference call, and he was moving on to inventing the prototype for touch tone dialing. In the meantime, my mom and him are broke.

I remember saying to him, "They all say they're the guy, Dad. You know, they're connected to the big man and all that nonsense." Even so, I went to meet this guy with my father. Turns out, the guy was Anthony, but I wasn't getting who he was yet.

I guess I was feeling like a big shot that day, and I says, "So my father's telling me you're the man. Is that what you're telling him? You're the big guy? Who are you with? Who are you connected to?"

Without hesitation, Anthony slammed his fists on the table, and he tells me to come closer. "You see, son, I'm not sure what you mean by connected. You know, my hand is connected to my wrist, and my wrist is connected to my arm, and my arm is connected to my shoulder. Is that what you're talking about? I'm connected that way. Is that what you're asking me?" No question, I knew I was looking at the man. He made the others look like schoolboys.

I'm thinking, *I'm going to connect myself with this guy—get made, sworn into La Cosa Nostra, get my button.* Soon thereafter, I did get connected with Anthony, and it's always been amazing to me that I made that connection through my father. Once again, it was all about the black box. My dad made the mistake of providing Anthony with a modified version of the black box. He put that one in a blue box, and naturally, it was called the "blue box."

If you were arrested with the black box, it was an automatic five years. But that was only if it was active. Anthony had said to him, "Walter, I can't take it when it's active. Once the battery is in it, it works, and I can't take it like that."

So my dad made the pads work with a magnet. It would only work if you put the magnet on it; then it would activate. You would carry the magnet in one pocket, and you would carry the unit in your other pocket. They couldn't charge you for that. Nevertheless, getting involved in that again would come back to haunt him.

I'm not trying to hide anything about my father here. Like I said in the beginning, I'm not writing our memoirs the way Will Rogers described them. I've been a very bad guy and harmed a lot of people, but my dad was just making harmless mistakes in judgment. Deciding to provide Anthony with a modified version of the black box was another one of them, but he was just looking for a way to take care of his family. It wasn't about the money with him. He wasn't looking to put himself in a million-dollar house. My parents weren't that way. I think the most my dad ever saw at one time in his life was $50,000.

Turns out that during the time my father hooked up with Anthony, he also borrowed some money from him. I found that out when Anthony came by my house to collect it. He tells me, "Your dad owes us money, Thiel."

"That's my dad owing you money," I tell him. "I don't owe you any money."

And he says, "I'm not going to come into the house. I'm going to go over to the tree and take a leak, and when I come back, I'm going to hold you up by your ankles. Everything that falls out is mine, or you can do the right thing and pay what your dad owes. The choice is going to be yours." That's the way Anthony talked. He talked in riddles, in metaphors.

Anthony thought too much of my father to go to him directly. My dad had borrowed the money from him, but Anthony knew what I was, and how I made my money. He knew my dad didn't have it, and he knew the chances of my dad ever paying him back were slim. That's the way he gave it to him. You know, my dad needed it, he borrowed it, but Anthony says, "I don't have the heart to hurt him, so I'm coming to you. Pay your dad's debt." And I did, which my father never knew.

The difference between my dad and me was this: He was just looking for his due, and I was out to hurt people. I was looking for all that the devil had to offer, and when you do that, it's hard to get your soul back.

At the beginning of my cat burglar days, 1969.

CHAPTER FIFTEEN

"I was and still am the best jewel thief."
—Peter J. Salerno

When I crossed the line, I knew I wasn't going back, and I also knew I didn't want to be just another soldier, another guy, another driver. I didn't want to be just anything. If I was going to engage in a life of crime, it wasn't my plan to be a garden variety crook. It was all about rising to the pinnacle of that world, the underworld. I was going to be the best career criminal there ever was, and before long, I was looking to move on from what I'd been doing. There had to be better ways to be an earner.

There are many facets to organized crime, and when Anthony took me in, he gave me my criminal career options. He says, "If you're going to choose a profession, I'd like to see you go into jewel thieving, but who knows if you'll make it? If not, you may have to go the way I have always had to go." Anthony was known for extortion.

There is an interesting twist to burglary as a profession: You hide behind the mask; nobody ever sees your face. Extortion, loan sharking, and bookmaking—those are all done with your face. Anthony went on to say, "You're going to limit your ability to keep getting away, but if you hide behind the mask, who is going to identify you? As a matter of fact, Thiel, when you go to give somebody a beating, always wear a mask. That way, they can never say in court, 'I was beat up by So-and-so.' The first thing a prosecutor's gonna say is, 'Can you identify him?' Wear a mask, and that can't happen."

Being a jewel thief demanded a certain amount of respect, too, and I decided to go down that road. I didn't want to be just another jewel thief, either. I wanted to excel, and I have to admit it, I was trained by one of the best.

Pete Salerno is the guy. There's no doubt about it. I don't care what Dominick Latella, his brother-in-law and original partner, has to say about the subject, Pete was the guy—a very astute jewel thief. He was athletic and agile, a great cat burglar and proud of it. Pete was definitely one of the best there was, but he was a wicked soul, and I mean that. There is nothing nice about Pete Salerno. The man has a real career criminal mentality, and he has no mercy for anybody.

When Steve Kroft interviewed him for *60 Minutes* back in 2005, he asked him, "Have you reformed, Pete?"

Pete said, "No comment," which means he would still be robbing people if he was out today, and he is close to seventy. Pete went on to say, "I was and still am the greatest jewel thief." These days, he's sitting in jail.

Pete Salerno didn't come up with the idea of stealing from people while they were home. He learned everything he knew from Frank Bova, a veteran of World War II, who was trained in reconnaissance by the United States government in the Office of Strategic Services (OSS). In fact, Frank Bova led the Ranger team that broke into the Gestapo and robbed the Nazis of some of their plans.

When Bova came back to the States, one thing led to another, and he found himself getting involved with New York City's criminal element. As a favor to Pete, who was getting a reputation on the street in the 1950s, a friend introduced him to Bova, who taught him everything he needed to know about the burglary business. Pete spent a year robbing people with Frank. He was learning from the best, but an apprentice doesn't make any money. They could have a $50,000 score, and Bova would hand him three hundred bucks. In the beginning, though, it wasn't about the money for Salerno; it was all about the education.

Pete put together a second-generation team, which was dubbed the Dinner Set Gang. He had married an Italian girl named Gloria Savino, whose father, John Savino, had a brother-in-law connected to the mob, none other than Frank Sacco. When Dominick Latella married Gloria's twin, Sandra Savino, he hooked up with Pete. Salerno trained two other brother-in-laws, Pat and Ray, but they weren't suited for the work. Pete told Pat not to run one time, but he ran across a yard anyway, hit an empty pool, fell in and was knocked out. Jewel thievery didn't work out for Pat and Ray. So Pete was the leader of the Dinner Set Gang, and initially they kept it in the blood. They all worked with relatives, but Frank Sacco opened the door for me.

I'm not writing a book about the Dinnertime Burglars. The magazines, the TV shows and other books have covered that. You can go to the Internet and find all kinds of things about us. That's not what this is about; it's just part of the story.

As it goes, I was introduced to Pete while I was running money back and forth from Miami to New York. Carl Miller had told Sacco I was crazy. "He's got no fear," he told him, and in 1968, Frank arranged for me to be introduced to Pete at a mob warehouse in Opa-locka, Florida.

After the Sacco trial and hiding out in Ocala with my family, I met up with Pete again. I was looking for work, and he took me in. I wasn't sure I was going to be a good burglar. Nobody knew, but I adapted. Pete knew I had it, and I proved it. You have to be well-suited to cat burglary, and I found out I could do what was required of me to succeed. I'm just saying that I blended in. I could run, I could jump and I had a brain. I remember Pete telling me, "If you do exactly what I say, I'll teach you how to be a cat burglar."

One of the first things I learned was what we needed to have with us to do a job. Of course, we wore all black: black slacks, black tops, black ski masks, black gloves and black Clark's Wallabees, shoes that are known for leaving no treads. We also had a bag of tools with us, and we took the same things every time we went out robbing people.

The most important thing in the bag was the pry bar, which we used for cracking window panes and wedging safes from walls. Penlights worked as our light source and as signaling devices. We also used alligator clips to bypass alarms and buck knives to cut screens and moldings on windows and doors. It was also important to have some cash on us if we missed our driver. You might think leather gloves are best for burglarizing, but garden gloves are thinner and give you better sensitivity. Gum helps with dry mouth, and you can't signal a partner with a dry mouth. Rope and grappling hooks were needed for climbing, and flathead screwdrivers were in the bag if we needed to get precise in a break-in.

At the end of each night, all the tools went back in the bag, and the bags were always discarded in a body of water. We got rid of the bags every night. You don't want any evidence from a job, and it's the driver's job to get rid of the bag.

My first job came along in December 1969. At that time, Pete was the break-in guy, John Donaldson was our driver, and Dominick Latella, whom I called Don, and I were the lookouts. Within six months, though, Pete was taking me inside the houses. I can honestly say I was never scared—never. Oh yeah, you might sweat, but I was never nervous about anything happening in one of the houses. The nerves come with thinking you might get caught on the outside. And if you got away, that was your reward. Pete threw me some chump change on my first night out.

The idea to break into houses when the people are at home came from Frank Bova. He decided to rob people when they were home eating dinner. You go in when they're eating dinner because they're distracted, and the rich don't eat like we do. It's a lot like it is in the movies. They're all congregated in one area, with the maids, the butlers, everybody around them, focusing on them.

And the stuff we're looking for is upstairs unguarded. A woman's not going to be wearing her best pieces at home with her husband. The best stuff is upstairs in the master bedroom.

Back when I was robbing, rich people were using safe deposit boxes to store their good jewelry, and, of course, through the years we started hooking up with girls who were in charge of those at the banks. Pete was very introverted unless you knew him. Don was a playboy, but he wasn't cunning about how to cultivate those kinds of relationships. So I was the one who always thought that way. That was my doing.

Anyway, people had their jewelry in their safe deposit boxes, and the good stuff came out for dinner functions or galas. You can understand that they wanted to be wearing their best pieces on those occasions. If they bring it home from the bank on Thursday or Friday, it goes back on Monday. That means it's all going to be in the house on the weekend, and it's going to be in the master bedroom and dressing area.

So we targeted the weekend events. We'd read about big party events, balls and fundraisers, and we'd go to those and try to mingle with the rich. The wealthy fences received invitations to those, too, and they would invite us along sometimes. The fence, of course, was our jeweler, and most rich people are used to using a certain jeweler, too. I can remember attending some of the galas. The point was to see who was wearing what. We actually tracked the social calendar in an area we were planning to hit.

There were times when a big event came around during the week, but we usually hit our targets on Thursdays through Sundays. We only worked three months a year, from six to ten o'clock at night. That's why we could have other business interests during the rest of the year. We'd come out in October, November and December, and sometimes in January, and then we were done until the next year. To be working in the dark from Florida to Boston, it had to be that way.

Pete was so good at what we were doing that he could price the stuff, and he could fence it, too. He taught me that the Smithsonian was the way to learn how to price things. That was the place to study gems, and I was required to take a Smithsonian gemology correspondence course to learn the Four C's: cut, color, clarity and carat. When I later left Pete to form my own gang, I was able to price my own stuff. I didn't need any help anymore, and I always knew exactly what I was looking for.

Eventually, I found out that Pete and Don were cheating me. Case in point: the DuPont score. This was back in January 1973, and I was the driver on the boat that night. We were looking to hit some oceanfront property on Juno Beach. It wasn't until it was all over that we realized we'd hit the heir to the DuPont fortune. Pete and Don had a twelve million dollar take, and just like my first night out with them, they threw me chump change on that one.

If we scored under $100,000, we used a fence in Hallandale, Florida. Anything over $100,000 needed to be fenced in New York. Wally Gans made out on the 47th Street Diamond Exchange. We usually got a third of the dollar value. This was the guy who was making duplicates of Elizabeth Taylor's jewelry for people, and he paid us in cash. When we weren't planning on working one night, Pete and I flew to New York, fenced the jewels, and had more money than we could spend. It was all about the money back then.

Because of the greed that set in, knowing that Salerno wasn't giving me my share after the fence, I went off and formed my own group. I remember walking out of Pete's house one night, and I said to him, "Burn in hell."

Anthony knew I could cut it on my own. He says to me, "You've never needed Pete." Pete and Don knew I had formed my own team. I didn't need them, and I proved it many times over. It was time for a third-generation group, and I made the break with Pete and Don in 1974.

Shelly and Randy Shaw in Hollywood, Florida, 1973.

*"There was never going to be a Christmas in my house
without a tree and lots of gifts."*

CHAPTER SIXTEEN

"Their gang was the most sophisticated one I've ever seen."
—Detective Dan Riemer

By the time I left Pete and Don, I was training three new guys to work with me: Dale McClain, McClain's uncle, Marshall Perlow, and a friend of his, Gene Tyce. Donaldson came with me, too. McClain was only sixteen, and Perlow and Tyce were twenty-one and nineteen. Being younger than me, I could tell they were looking at me like I was some kind of hero. I taught those kids everything I know about the burglary business.

We went a week between jobs before we started planning our targets, so I never had any trouble with hitting the same houses as Pete. That didn't happen. There are too many houses for that to happen. I would always read the newspaper to find out about any criminal activity in an area, and if any burglaries were committed the papers would start saying what kind of burglaries. If they said it happened at dinnertime, then I knew it was Pete, and I'd leave. The area was heated up then, and I didn't want any part of that. I didn't want to be blamed for their earlier jobs.

It wasn't like we were hitting just one house a night, either. Unless I saw that what I had taken was enough for me not to risk another job, I'd go for two, three or more in a night. If it's not a big enough payday, I have to go for more. I want to make fifty, sixty, a hundred thousand that night. I'm not going to go out and risk it for five thousand dollars. It's just not worth it. I've got two or three guys I gotta pay, so I'm going to go in where I know it's going to be worthwhile.

In my crew, the driver got 20 percent, and my partners and I split the rest evenly. The guy going in the house doesn't get more than the lookout. I believed we were all taking the same risk.

What we did was this: When we made it into the master bedroom, we took the pillowcases off their pillows and dumped the
whole jewelry box in there. I mean the whole box. That was most
of the time, and we called the pillowcases "Glad bags." Obviously,
there was no time to sort through the stuff while we were still in
the house. When we were done for the night, the guys would give
their pillowcases to me, they'd go drink, change or whatever
they're going to do that night, and they'd leave me with the stuff
to separate it. The leader gets to sort it. I know what's real and
what isn't real.

Also, by doing it that way, the guys have no evidence on me.
Because they hadn't seen any of it, they can't say what was stolen
from a particular house. You know, "I remember an eight-carat
marquis diamond coming from..." Nobody gets to see the stuff. I
learned that from Pete. "Give them their end, but don't let them
see it. You don't want them to identify it and put you away," he
said. So I went by those old rules.

When I trained my team, Dale, Marshall and Gene, I had definite rules. One of them usually surprises people. That's the one
about anything that looked sentimental. The spiel was that anything that's sentimental goes back or gets left. You got two choices: Don't take it, or send it back. Locks of hair, baby teeth and baby
pictures—anything that looked significant to a mother goes back.

Remember the way it was at Halloween? You'd go all around
the neighborhood and collect candy; then you sorted it when you
got home. That's what I did. I dumped it all out, and I sorted it. If
I found stuff that was significant, that was irreplaceable, that was
not a piece of jewelry and was sentimental to a mother, and if I
knew the address, it had to go back. That was just me. Not everybody felt that way.

One year, we did a house two nights before Christmas, and
one of my partners went downstairs and took the little packages

underneath the tree. I was livid. We got back to my house, and I said, "They gotta go back."

He said, "Are you crazy? You don't go back to the scene of a crime, Walt."

"If they're home, then we're going to jail, because these are going back." And we took them back. That's just the way I believed. I mean, you know, it's bad enough you're raping them on their jewelry, but it's worse to take something they can't replace. That's just my philosophy. It doesn't make it right; it doesn't make it wrong; it's just the way I believe. If I could take it back, I would take it back.

I remember when Dale put a little dog in the refrigerator one time, and I went back to let it out that same night. Again, that doesn't make me a hero, but I got a soft spot. Another rule: I never carried a weapon.

It was also important to me that we never did a house with kids in it. I've got a ski mask on, and they'll never forget that. If they saw some stranger creeping around wearing a ski mask, they would never go to sleep feeling safe in that room again. That would be a horrible thing to do to a kid. Why would I want to do that? What amount of money is that worth? I'm not doing that house for any amount of money. They could tell me that Sinbad's jewelry was in the bedroom, and I'm not going in if kids are in the house. I wouldn't take that chance. It wasn't worth it to me. I know that doesn't make me a good guy, but I had children, too, and I always wanted them to feel safe. If children are sitting at the dinner table, it's a pass.

Obviously, we walked away from more houses than we hit. If we counted up all the houses we were going to do that we didn't do, it would be in the tens of thousands. Ten or twelve thousand would be my guess. They weren't situated right, or they didn't have the stuff, or we'd trigger an alarm, or we stepped on a pad in the yard and lights went on. There were a lot of variables that could make us quit on a target. We just had to walk.

I trained all my men that "there's another day. Just because you don't get the score tonight, doesn't mean that tomorrow won't come. But it won't come if you make a mistake going in on the wrong night."

Back with Pete's group, the FBI always labeled us "master jewel thieves." They actually called us the "Cartier of jewel thieves." We were definitely known as the cream of the crop in our profession, and that continued for my group. No matter the generation, we all used the same modus operandi, robbing rich people while they were eating dinner at home. If Bova was the originator of the Dinnertime Burglars, Salerno was the second generation, and my new group would be the third. We were all "Dinnertime Burglars."

When I walked into a group of criminals—my peers—I used to hear this said, "He's one of the top jewel thieves in the country." They might go on to say, "And if you give him a beating, you have to kill him." That's what I had said to Carl back at the warehouse in 1968, and it was known on the street. In other words, you don't give him a beating and walk away. You have to kill him first. I got what I wanted by saying that to Carl. He spread the word. It is not easy to admit that my life has been a failure in the eyes of the legitimate world, but I achieved my mark among my peers.

Pete Salerno is in jail now, and I hear Don is doing a book. His book will be all about the great jobs we did. I don't want to be singled out with one job; I don't want to be known as the DuPont score, or the Liberace score. I don't need all that now. I think Pete and Don are in the mindset of being the greatest, and I'm not of that mindset anymore. Being called the "greatest" jewel thief elevates crime. "Greatest" means something good.

I don't want to be known in that vein, as the greatest. If I did want to go in that vein, I could say that I've never been caught in a job. They can beat their chests, but they were caught in several jobs, and they both went to jail for that. My guys knew that if I took them on a score we weren't going to get caught. I was ratted on, circumstantial. They may have suspected me in every robbery case, but they could never prove anything. And I'm not admitting to anything.

I don't need to be waving red flags on the jobs I did. I will win the case because it is called freedom of speech, but to go out and blatantly admit to certain jobs that I went to prison for, or was suspected of, I don't want to do that. Why take the shot? Pete and Don still want the accolades.

When I was interviewed in 2005 by Steve Kroft for *60 Minutes,* I distanced myself from Pete and Don. And when I found out that they were interviewed for the same piece, I said, "I want out of the show. Get me out, or I'll sue you." And, of course, knowing that I meant it, they cut me from the show. I don't want to be linked with Pete Salerno and Dominick Latella in any kind of way. I broke with them too many years ago for that. Nevertheless, they're part of my story.

So I proved myself as a jewel thief, and I wasn't giving it up, but I was looking for another angle on making money.

CHAPTER SEVENTEEN

"Then you're just a cowboy? You think you can rob anybody?"
—Johnny "Potatoes," Mafia Soldier

My first job with Pete had been in December 1969, and I got into those velvet paintings at the flea market in the fall of 1971. I was still out robbing people at nighttime, but I was also working a day job. As I've mentioned, the Dinnertime Burglars only worked three months a year, from six to ten at night. It had to be dark outside for us to pull off a job. We had alternate business interests during the other nine months.

After the flea market, I opened up a company called Archie's Pants in Hollywood, Florida. I still had some of the paintings, too, which would come close to getting me killed. By that time, Connie and I had our two kids, and I had bought us a house on Hood Street. Salerno was living around the corner on Johnson Street.

Unless I was hiding out somewhere, everybody knew how to reach me—I'm talking about the wise guys. During that time, I went by the name of Archie Lewis. My dad didn't want his name associated with who I was, so I took the name of Archie, my beloved pseudo-uncle. This was before "truth day." I used one of my dad's middle names, Lewis, as my last name. Remember, my dad's full name was Walter Harvey Lewis Charles Shaw. So my monogram on the street was Archie Lewis, and that's the way the racket guys started to know me. That was my name for collections, extortions, whatever.

As it goes, these four guys come down from New York one day, but they say they're from Georgia. They go to my house, which is unorthodox—can't do that, against the rules—but that's what saved my life. Connie was very clever about the world where I come from. These guys said to her, "We're looking for Archie." That was a big mistake on their part, but that's what saved me.

That day she calls and says to me, "I've got three guys in the house and another one's out in their car. They're looking for you, for Archie. They want to know who would know how to give them a price on some paintings." In other words, because of the name they're calling me she's letting me know that something ain't right.

I tell her, "Put the ringleader on the phone." So she does, and this guy's name is Johnny, Johnny "Potatoes." Good-looking, handsome guy, Johnny gets on the phone.

He says, "I've got some paintings on velvet, and I heard you used to have those. I want to see if you can give me a price on them, or maybe you'll buy them off me."

"Look, that's my house." And, of course, I hear Connie's mouth going in the background.

She's telling them, "Hey, Archie and I are separated. We're going through a divorce. He doesn't even live here anymore." She wants those guys out of there.

So Johnny says, "Oh, I didn't know that."

"Yeah," I tell him, "we're getting a divorce. I've got a clothing store over in Hollywood. Come over to the store; it's on Hollywood Circle." I'm trying to get him over where I'm at, away from my wife and kids. Connie's keeping her cool, but I know she's terrified. So they leave, and they come over to my shop. I have Donaldson with me all the time and he was there, too.

Of course, Donaldson's got the gun in the bag when they get there, and I put him at the end of the counter. The three of them come in, and the other guy stays in the car. I never did see him, but they come in and Johnny says, "Listen, Archie, we got a truckload of paintings, and…"

I said, "What name did you call me?"

"Archie. Isn't your name Archie?"

"Yeah," I tell him. Again, his calling me that saved me. When I did the painting deal a couple of years before this, an extortion deal, it wasn't under Archie, it was under Walter Shaw.

"We heard you deal in these things," he says to me.

"I did at one time, years ago, you know."

He says, "We've got a truckload of them. Will you meet us to talk about it?"

"Yeah; I'll meet you," I tell him. "How about meeting in Hallandale? There's a Denny's over there." Now, Hallandale, at that time, was under wise guys' protection with the police department. Some of the cops were on the take.

"Yeah, we'll meet at Denny's, 9 o'clock tonight."

"I'll be there," I said. "Are all you guys coming?"

"Just the three of us," he answered me. I'm thinking then about the fourth guy.

"I'll see you there at nine," I tell him.

I found out later that they'd been in a mob restaurant in Hallandale just days before, Doria's Italian Restaurant, and they were looking for me there. That, too, saved my life. The four of them were at the bar talking about how they were down from New York to do a hit on a guy.

The bartender was a rat, and he calls the cops to report some suspicious guys in town to do a hit. He tells them they've got Georgia tags, and the police ran a check to find out who the tags belonged to. Johnny "Potatoes" turns out to be a soldier from the Funzi Tieri family. They were down looking for payback or to finish me off for the paintings I'd lifted.

My guy, Donaldson, is also named John, and we went to Denny's to the meeting that night. Because it was a public place, we left our guns in the car. We're inside, and, naturally, when they meet me, they embrace me. You know, they shake my hand, give me one of those Italian hugs, but they were just checking to see if we had weapons on us.

So we sit down, and Johnny's across from me. He starts to say something, and I says, "Look, let's cut to the chase. You're not here for paintings. You're not here for anything but to size me up. You made a mistake by going to my house today, but we're going to let that go. What do you want?"

He asks, "Who you with?"

"What do you mean, who am I with? I'm not with anybody. I'm with me. My hand's connected to my wrist, my wrist to my elbow, my elbow to my shoulder, and I'm the boss of my household." That's what Anthony always said, "I'm the boss of my household."

He says, "You sure?"

"I'm positive," I tell him.

"Well, you owe a guy in Georgia for that truckload of paintings you grabbed."

I asked him again, "What do you want?"

"We want the money," he tells me.

"I don't give anything back," I answered.

He says, "You don't give nothin' back?"

"No."

"Then you're just a cowboy? You think you can just rob anybody?" he says to me.

I says, "I ain't givin' nothin' back. Do what you gotta do, and go see who you gotta see, but I ain't givin' nothin' back."

"All right," he says, "I guess the meeting's over." And we go outside.

I'm out front then with Donaldson, and Johnny says to me, "Where do you want it?" He's got one of his guys holding the gun.

I says, "Right here, tough guy."

Donaldson's standing there listening to this dialogue, getting a little nervous, and he says, "Are you out of your mind?" I don't answer him, and I'm keeping my eye on Johnny.

"Hey, Johnny, you ain't got the guts to do it? You're gonna have your flunky do it for you?" I said.

He says, "Yeah, because you're nobody."

"Look, if I was somebody, I would do you myself. I don't need nobody to pull the trigger for me." Donaldson's freaking out with all this, and the guy hands Johnny the gun to finally do me.

When the guy hands Johnny the gun, the plan was to walk me over to the car and have the fourth guy come out of the trunk to do me. Instead, Donaldson embraces Johnny, and then we had a gun.

So Johnny says to me, "You're with somebody, aren't you?"

"Yeah, I'm with somebody."

"I had a feeling you were," he says. "Who are you with?" And I tell him I'm with Anthony. Only when I was in a corner did I use his name, and Johnny's eyes got real big. "I guess we got a problem," he says. Of course, because I'm protected, he knows that threatening me could cost him his life.

When he told me he was with Funzi, I agreed, saying, "Yeah, we definitely got a problem."

He says, "I f...in' knew it. I knew you were with somebody."

"And you broke the rules."

"We didn't know who you were," he says, looking for an excuse.

"I don't care if you knew or not. You broke the rules. I didn't go to your house. I'd have come to you," I told him.

Anyway, the cops ended up surrounding us, and we were all arrested. I mean, they just laid down on us. It seems that the fourth guy got locked inside the automatic release trunk, and a Denny's customer heard him thumping on the inside. The customer called the cops, and they're all over. We didn't know that. None of us knew that. One of the cops opens the trunk of Johnny's dark brown Continental and finds the fourth guy lying there with a .32-caliber revolver in one hand and a .12 gauge sawed off shotgun in the other.

When we got to the jail they separated us. They found a

hundred grand on them—twenty-five grand apiece to hit me, and I tell the cop, who's working with us, "I want to speak to Johnny."

It didn't matter that we were in jail; I knew we were going to a sit-down. He had told me who he was with, and I knew his boss wasn't going to give him up. So I walk over to the cell, and I says, "Johnny, I'm letting you all go. You get your car back, you get your money back, but the cops ain't gonna give us back our guns. You're getting everything but the guns."

He says, "Really?"

"Yeah," I tell him.

Johnny looks at me and says, "I guess we picked the wrong guy."

CHAPTER EIGHTEEN

"Are you with anybody?"
—Eddie Perrone, Bondsman

Being connected is what it's all about in the mob, especially in a beef. A beef is a bad situation, like the one with Johnny Potatoes, but I had one at my house one time that would later have me crawling into the trunk of a car for the first and last time.

A guy named Eddie Perrone was with the Columbo crew, and he was a button guy, a made member of the Mafia. Turns out, Eddie wanted to buy some jewelry from me. I had a big score, about $75,000, and I had him come to my house to do the deal. Because you only use the name when you're in trouble, Eddie didn't know that I was with Anthony. I was told that you don't just tell people, you keep them guessing. Until you're backed into a corner, you don't tell nobody you're with anybody.

So Eddie came to my house, and he was going to buy the package from me. Two of my men were out front. I've got a 5,000-square-foot house at the time, and Eddie's back in the master bedroom with me. The stuff is all laid out, and he says, "What do you want for this?"

"Seventy-five thousand," I tell him.

He always wore a pocket book—the fashion back then—and he says, "Are you with anybody?"

"No, I'm not with anybody," I told him.

"Then why should I pay you?"

I says, "Because you want to buy the jewelry. That's how it works."

"I'll give you twenty thousand," he comes back at me.

"I don't want $20,000. There is $250,000 laying here on the bed, and I want $75,000."

Eddie pulls out a gun and says, "Well, I'm just gonna take it."

"You saw my men," I reminded him.

"I know," he says, "and we'll have a blast getting out of your house."

That's when you pull a name out, and I told him I was with Anthony. He looks at me and says, "Anthony?"

"Yeah, there's only one Anthony in this town," I tell him.

He says, "Get him on the phone."

So I dialed the number and gave him the receiver. Anthony's wife answers, and Eddie knows then that I'm with Anthony. He says to her, "I made a mistake. Tell Anthony I'm sorry, and I'll call him back tomorrow."

Eddie looks at me and says, "So I made a mistake."

I says, "I'll see you tomorrow."

"What do you mean you'll see me tomorrow?"

I says, "You think this is going to be the end of it? You did this. Did I do this? Did I come to your house and stick you up? You came to my house, I invited you in for safety, knowing the cops couldn't bust us or anything, and you want to stick me up? You got a problem. I'll see you tomorrow."

So I told Anthony, and he says, "Okay, we'll split what he was supposed to pay you."

"Fine," I tell him.

When we went to the sit-down, Eddie says, "Anthony, I didn't know."

"You didn't know? He told you, didn't he?"

"Yeah," he says.

"Give us the money," Anthony tells him.

So he pulled out the money he needed to pay me for the jewelry, Anthony and I split it, I keep the package, and Eddie looks at me and says, "I got this one marked down, kid. He can't live forever." That's what he says to me. Anthony's ten years older than me.

"Mark it down. I don't care. You did wrong. I didn't do it," I tell him. Marked down meant that I had made an enemy, and months later, Eddie puts me in the trunk of a car.

When I was coming up, I was being schooled that you're not really made until you're forty. In fact, Anthony told me, "Not many get made."

"Yeah," I said, "Why's that?"

"Because most of you don't make it to forty," he told me.

He was right about that, and because of the way I was out there, I probably never would have seen forty. You gotta live through a lot to get to that stage, but I knew I could get made if I lived long enough. Prison saved me though. I was uncontrollable, not going by anybody's rules or laws. Starting with the $96,000, I broke rules. I thought I was above their law. Sometimes I even used another one of Anthony's lines: "We don't do sit-downs."

CHAPTER NINETEEN

"Nothing personal, guys, it's just business."
—Walter T. Shaw

Even by the time I walked out on Pete, I was finding burglary to be too physically demanding. I'm only twenty-six at the time, but I was looking for easier ways to score. Just like my dad, I was always chasing dollars. Difference is, he was chasing what should have been his anyway.

In March of that year, Donaldson and I were cashing some bad checks at a bank in North Miami Beach, and the vice president of the bank was onto us. He brings the security guard around to arrest us, and in walks David Hatterman, a detective who'd been after me for a long time.

"You're getting booked for grand theft, Shaw. You're busted," he tells me.

"You ain't booking me for nothin'," I tell him.

Hatterman says, "There's a millionaire in New York who thinks differently. He's missing four personal checks."

We walk out to my Mark IV, he pops the trunk and finds two unregistered Browning .9 millimeters. Hatterman laughs in my face, telling me I'm going away for a long time. I laugh back, telling him I'd buy him some doughnuts and coffee across the street in a couple of hours.

In my favor, the millionaire from New York decided not to press charges. It was too much trouble to fly down to Florida. The state prosecutor had failed to tell Hatterman those details, and I walked out of the courtroom. Hatterman's going nuts, and I says to him, "Time for a doughnut and some coffee?"

There was too much money in robbery to give it up, though, and I put my new team together after that nonsense. With burglary, it was all tax-free cash, no deposits, no records and no banks. I knew I couldn't beat the cash flow, and I was back in business.

My guys were good, and we pulled off hundreds of jobs without a hitch. On January 15, 1975, however, the luck would run out. A young kid would get killed on a job.

Bill Smith was an ironworker, a legitimate kid just trying to provide for his family. He'd been laid off, was in debt and needed something extra. Bill and his wife had a new baby, and I finally agreed to take him out on a job, but I put him with Dale and Gene that night. Because I was planning to meet Salerno later on, I didn't go out with them.

I showed McClain an easy target, and Tyce would drive him and Smith to Tamarac. Turns out the cops were staked out when they got there. Things went bad, and thinking it was me, the cops blew Smith away that night. Gene and Dale were arrested, and the cops separated them. The detectives twisted the law that night by telling them that a death taking place during the commission of a crime could be blamed on anyone involved in the crime. Both were told they'd be charged with murder if they didn't cooperate by talking about me. Gene folded, but Dale stood up, refused to talk, and he asked to make the only phone call you're allowed at a time like that.

I'll never forget his call to me that night. Dale calls me up and says, "Get the stuff out of your house, Walt, Gene's talking. Bill's dead. The cops killed him."

From various law enforcement officers, there have been plenty of innuendos through the years that I'd been set up for that. I knew too much, and it was a good way to get rid of me. I figured it all out from prison. I had never understood how the police knew where the gang was going that night, and I knew it had to have come from the inside. Somebody else knew that I was going out with my group before I met up with Pete. Instead of doing what they thought I was doing, I went out robbing people in my local neighborhood with Pete's nephew. Bill got himself killed because I chose to stay in the immediate area that night.

It's been talked about in a variety of media interviews that Salerno had flipped. He made a deal, and he knew that I knew he was talking. Ironically, I was supposed to roll him over—tell my boss that Pete was going to the other side—but I didn't. I was too close to Pete to do that to him.

Connie went with me to tell Linda, Bill's wife, that Bill was dead. She actually went with Linda to identify Bill. That night she said to me, and I'll never forget it, "Now you know what I used to go through every time you walked out the door. I didn't know whether I was going to bond you out or identify you." That's exactly how she said it—exactly. "Will you stop now, Thiel?"

I knew I wasn't stopping, and I needed to get to Tyce. When I learned later that day that Gene was talking about Salerno, too, I knew I was really in trouble. About a week or so later, a fleet of police cars forced Donaldson and me off the highway on I-95, and they were all armed with shotguns. I was booked on Gene's testimony.

That was my second major arrest. The first had been before Bill Smith was killed. In that one, Salerno and I were trying to pick up an easy score on a cocaine deal. Neither of us was interested in drug trafficking, but we'd been offered $300,000 to pull off a purchase of coke. The two Chicago racketeers involved in the deal turned out to be with the Broward County Sheriff's Office, and we were charged with possession, distribution and sale of cocaine at the scene. Sitting in the squad car, one of the detectives says to me, "You're finally going to jail, Shaw."

There wasn't just one nemesis in the police force trying to stop me. There was a task force of about forty guys assigned to the job. When I was arrested, they told me, "We've spent a lot of taxpayer money on you. As a matter of fact, we have twenty-four-hour surveillance on you."

The cops were staked outside my house in Emerald Hills one time, and, of course, they were trying not to be obvious. They were sitting in their van, and I walked out there with some coffee and doughnuts. I said, "I'll see you in the morning; I'm going to bed now."

I was never mad at anybody for trying to catch me. If I got sloppy, shame on me. My whole game was to get away, and theirs was to catch me. "Good luck"—that's the way I approached them. Through the years, my favorite saying whenever I spoke to one of them was always, "Nothing personal, guys, it's just business." That later came back on me, though.

Anyway, Donaldson and I were taken to the Hollywood, Florida, jail after being arrested on I-95. On the strength of Tyce's storytelling, I was charged with breaking and entering. I had no problem posting the $6,500 bond, and I never thought a jury would buy the testimony of a kid anyway. Tyce was just nineteen at the time. Turns out, him being my driver, he took them to a lake where he'd dropped at least fifty bags. Like I said, that was the driver's duty, and Tyce took them to the bags when he ratted me out.

I was arrested a few weeks later on another charge of breaking and entering. The police had looked at every burglary Gene was talking about for a possible conviction on me, and I was arrested for those one at a time. There were four of them. A federal charge of counterfeiting was a fifth arrest, and the sixth charged me with conspiracy to distribute cocaine, another federal charge. I had posted bond on the first five, but I had to turn to Eddie Perrone for the sixth. You'll remember Eddie Perrone, the bondsman.

After Eddie came through for me, knowing that I was facing hard time on the six cases against me, it's probably hard to believe that I turned to Pete to help me out. I needed some money to pay off Perrone and fund my lawyers, and Pete was also in need of some cash. By then, I had sold my house to pay my bonds and fund my attorneys, but Pete and I made some big scores, too. I threw Eddie my chump change on those. I kept ignoring him and not paying. That's why he showed up where I was staying and forced me into the trunk of his Continental. Standing right there behind the car, he says, "You can die right here or climb in and take a chance." I climbed in—the only time I spent in the trunk of a car—but I worked things out through Anthony again.

Anthony said, "Pay him, Thiel. You're in the wrong. You're trying to rob the guy. That's how he makes his gaff. This is his shtick, and you're trying to rob him. Just because you got away with it once doesn't mean you can do it twice, you know. You're in the wrong this time. Pay him his money." Once again, that's what comes from being connected.

Salerno and I were out robbing people up to the night before I was set to stand trial in 1975. Even then, I wasn't thinking they could put me away because of Tyce. *How could another burglar be a credible witness?* But the jury bought Gene's testimony, and I was convicted of first degree breaking and entering on June 15, 1975. That's when I turned around looking for Connie, and I see three rows of guys standing up wearing the same T-shirt. My face is printed on them, and the lettering says, "NOTHING PERSONAL, GUYS, IT'S JUST BUSINESS." The entire task force was there celebrating.

Federal District Court Judge Norman C. Roettger Jr. called me the "twentieth century highwayman, the modern day Jesse James." I actually saw those characterizations as accolades, as compliments, and the press ate it up. The *Miami Herald* printed his remarks the day after my sentencing hearing. It was all over the papers: *"Highwayman Gets Twenty."* That was good press, but it didn't matter anymore. Accolades mean nothing when you're looking at spending the rest of your life in prison. I was already on a sentence with the state, and I knew Roettger was getting ready to levy federal time on me. I'd been had.

Perlow had stood trial with me, and he was looking at prison time, too. Judge Weissing sentenced Marshall to thirteen years, and I was given fifteen. I got another fifteen-year sentence when the second case for breaking and entering was tried in Fort Lauderdale. I was acquitted of the state's charge for possession and conspiracy to distribute cocaine, but the feds convicted me of drug trafficking and I got twelve years. It was months before the other burglary trials were finished, but they cost me another seven years. Six trials netted me forty-nine years of hard time.

Unbelievably, eighteen months later, my dad gets four years in the federal system, the result of slipping again. On April 7, 1976, a headline in one of the Miami papers read: "Electronics Wizard Charged with Using 'Blue Box.'" My father was being tried on an eight-count federal indictment before a jury and U.S. District Court Judge James Lawrence King. According to Assistant U.S. Attorney David Geneson, "The FBI found that Shaw was 'bouncing off' long distance calls from the '800' sequence with the aid of an illegal device."

My father had hired Attorney Peter Aiken to defend him, and he responded to the charges by saying, "For many years, there has been a feud between Shaw and Ma Bell, and he has been threatened and harassed. There was no 'blue box.' There was a touchtone generator. Mr. Shaw is an inventor who was only testing his own touchtone generator to see if it was compatible with the Bell system."

On April 9, 1976, my dad was found guilty on all eight counts of using a "blue box" to circumvent long-distance telephone billing. He was sentenced to four years in federal prison for that, and he was going to the Federal Correctional Institution in Lexington, Kentucky. The following day, a headline in *The Miami News* read: "Phone Gyp Conviction Ordered."

Ironically, my father's attorney had argued back at his first sentencing hearing in 1965 that "a man with the know-how to invent burglar alarms and conference calls shouldn't be locked up." That could have saved both of us. I might not have been out robbing people, and my dad might have been out getting the money and recognition he was entitled to. Unfortunately, his attorney's argument hadn't worked.

My father and I may have been estranged, but we were about to be leading similar lives, both of them in prison, both of them tragic.

Electronics wizard charged with using 'blue box'

Headline in *The Miami News Reporter,* April 7, 1976.

"There was no blue box. What there was, was a touchtone generator."
—Peter Aiken, Defense Attorney

CHAPTER TWENTY

"Finality"
—Walter T. Shaw

In 1975, the year I went in, I was given a card, and on the card it said: "Release Date, Expiration of Sentence, 1996." So when an intake psychiatrist asked, "Now that you have come here and you know you're going to lockdown, what do you feel about that?"

"Finality," I told him.

"Finality. That's how you feel about being locked up?"

"Yeah," I said. "I know where I'm at. I know this is my life now. I'm here with you for the duration."

I served two terms, and for part of that time, I was being hunted. There wasn't any truth to it, which would come out later, but there was some suspicion that I was making a deal to talk, and by the first night I spent in jail, a contract was put on my life because of that. In fact, the first attempt on my life took place at the Fort Lauderdale Prison Annex. Fortunately, I was tipped off that some ground-up glass had been mixed in with my food.

Federal District Judge Roettger, the one who called me "a modern-day Jesse James," told me there was a contract on me. "Do you realize that you have $200,000 on your head?" he asked me in the courtroom. Except for one that might have come down the road because of Jimmy Hoffa disappearing like he did in July 1975, that was the highest contract in the United States at the time. Not that I wanted to be the guy with the highest contract, but I was, and I was just twenty-seven years old.

Early on, I was asked to put my family in the witness protection program, which provides protection for the witness and his family if the government is going to use that witness in a case concerning organized crime. But whatever may come, I wouldn't cooperate when it came down.

When I left the Fort Lauderdale Prison Annex, I was moved to Arcadia County Jail, and Connie and the kids moved over there to be near me. Even so, everybody in prison hits bottom. Nobody wants to live that way. I went that low six months after I was locked up. I really didn't care about going on at that point. I remember wanting everything in my life to stop.

Seeing how depressed I was, the prison officials put Marshall Perlow in my cell with me. The idea must have been that by him being in there I might keep it together. Nothing was helping me by that time, though. Even if it had been only one year, I expected to lose my wife over prison time. I knew I wasn't getting out, and I didn't want to face that day with her. That's why I chose that point to end my life. Beyond losing my freedom, the worst thing that could happen to me was losing my wife.

They give you a razor, a toothbrush and toothpaste as part of your kit when you get to prison. It was around 3:00 a.m. on December 14, 1975, and I went into the shower stall in our cell. I melted the razor out of the plastic and put it in a bar of soap. I did that to keep it steady and easy to hold. I was still in the Arcadia County Jail then.

I don't remember what time Marshall found me in there, but blood was everywhere, and the paramedics were called. I had slashed my wrists, and the doctor tells me nicely to cut the jugular the next time. My death wouldn't have been any loss to the prison system.

So I made it through my suicide attempt, and I went on to spend eleven years, six months and nine days behind bars. But there would be three more attempts on my life while locked up. Two of my cellmates at the Arcadia County Jail tried to hang me using a T-shirt. Those are cowboys who do it just for the reputation. They could say, "I killed Walter Shaw," like that's going to get them some points. That doesn't mean anything. There was some real stupidity among the prison population. Some of them didn't understand that it had to be an equal soldier to collect. A guy in the circle has to do you to collect the price on your head.

When it was real clear that I wasn't safe in the general population, the prison authorities started moving me around. From Arcadia, I was transferred to the Tarpon Springs Work Release Center. From there, a lieutenant from the Department of Corrections at Tallahassee traveled with me to North Sumter Correctional Institute. That was on January 28, 1976. By the time I got there, I'd been named John Simms to protect me, and they put me in a hospital wing isolation cell. Except for Connie's visits, I had no contact with anybody. I was losing my mind being in solitary confinement.

When the system finally realized I couldn't handle being alone, they transported me back to the Lake City Correctional Institute. Because of the threats on my life there, I was transferred a week later to the Tavares County Jail. I'm becoming a tourist in the Florida prison system. After Tavares, I went to Brevard County's correctional institution, and my mental condition wasn't getting any better. It was about that time that I learned about Connie's affair.

Back when I attempted suicide, I didn't know that Connie was having an affair, but I knew it was coming. I will never forget the moment my eight-year-old son told me that my wife was sleeping with somebody. I remember that explicitly. Right there in the visiting park, that was tough to hear from where I was sitting.

As it turned out, Connie was sleeping with her boss, who was fourteen years older and married with kids. My mother had caught her in bed with the guy, and she went nose to nose with him. She says, "You know, if my son was out, he'd kill you."

"Well, your son's not out," he tells her.

My mother answered, "That doesn't mean anything. He has friends."

The next time Connie came to see me, I says, "Let me tell you something. If you make a life with him, make sure you make it work. If you don't make it work, I'm killing him the day I get out of prison. You can let him know I'm coming. I don't care if it's twenty years from now, tell him I'm coming, and I'm doing it personally. I'm not sending anybody in my name, I'm coming myself. This face will be the last thing he sees."

I think Connie felt guilty about what she was doing. My parents had been supporting her with what little they had, and because her boss didn't want to deal with kids again, she had sent Randy and Shelly to live with them. Within a year, she woke up and realized what she was doing. That's when she took the kids back. My mom had asked me what to do about that, and I told her to return them to their mother.

I realized much later that I was responsible for what had happened. Connie was in the position she was in because of me, and I had done much worse things to her in our life together. Finally, when I was in prison, we were able to talk to each other about our marriage. Being on the other side of the bars, she was in a position to let it all hang out.

Sitting there in the visiting area, Connie said, "All those years I sat there waiting when you went out to rob people, and you'd come home with a Glad bag and a big smile on your face. You didn't realize that I was wondering every night if I was going to be like Linda Smith. You thought you were a hero, but you had no idea what you were doing to me, Thiel." (It is important to note here that Connie never looked at what I stole. She knew what I was doing was wrong.)

I asked, "Would you have told me this if I'd been on the street?"

She said, "No, I wouldn't have been worrying about what the kids were going to eat, either. You always found a way to provide for us; I never had to worry about that. Even though I knew you were breaking the law, I didn't want them to go through what you went through growing up. But they didn't deserve this life because of our stupid choices."

I may have been providing for them, but we never did anything normal as a family. Their mother did everything with our kids. She took them on picnics and outings with her sister's kids. I never went. Tired after a night out robbing people, doing things with the family bored me. I wanted to provide for them the life that I never had, but I didn't want to be bothered with any of the family stuff. I slept a lot in the daytime.

Connie loved me, though, and I didn't have to pay for that. Neil Sedaka wrote "The Hungry Years," and she sent a copy of that song to me in prison. Part of it reads, "I miss the hungry years/ The once upon a time/ The lovely long ago/ We didn't have a dime/ Those days of me and you/ We lost along the way.../ I miss the hungry years." I was crazy about Connie, no doubt about it.

In April 1976, as part of their ongoing effort to keep me alive behind bars, I landed on death row. The prison system put me in Lake Butler's K-Wing, one more place to protect me in solitary. When that happened, I asked the superintendent at Lake Butler to transfer me to DeSoto County. Even though I lived hunted, I wanted to be in the regular population. With them trying to protect me, I was literally losing my mind from being locked up so much. I didn't want to run from it anymore.

I told the warden and the head of the Department of Corrections, "Look, I want to go into a regular prison. You guys stay out of it. It's not your business. You don't understand it. It's not your world." It didn't matter then that Connie was cheating on me, I still wanted to see her, and DeSoto would do that for me.

"We have a duty to protect you," they told me. "That's part of our controlling your body in prison."

I agreed to go back into the population at my own risk, and they sent me to DeSoto Correctional Institution. On my second day there, an inmate tried to kill me with a metal pipe. There had been three attempts by then.

Connie and I still thought my appeal would go through when I was at DeSoto, and she wrote me a beautiful letter. She said, "Do you think we could still try, Thiel?" But the appeals were denied while I was there, and Connie and I lost our way together. I told her to get on with her life. After the third attempt on mine, they couldn't have me staying at DeSoto anyway, and I was transferred to the Florida State Penitentiary's East Unit. R-Wing, or death row, once again seemed to be the only place to keep me safe, but they put me on Q-Wing in the East Unit with the crazies. My wing became the holding cell for the death row inmates waiting to be executed. In fact, I could see "Old Sparky" from my cell.

When my appeals had been lost, Anthony asked my father to deliver a message to me in prison. My dad hadn't gone to prison in Kentucky yet. Anthony told me to die a soldier's death. Believing in where you come from is what dying a soldier's death is about. Believe you are a soldier. Believe that your cause, your oath, is the Mafia. My father was the messenger, but he didn't believe in the message. He said, "I hope you don't buy into all that nonsense, Thiel." Even then, he was still trying to set me straight.

I remember telling him, "I can't live day in and day out in prison, Dad. If he's worrying about what I may do or say in here, I might as well take his message to heart." Dying a soldier's death seemed kinder than prison life anyway, and I believed in orders, but after trying to kill myself the first time, I wasn't dying a soldier's death. I wasn't talking, either. I had a lot to think about, and plenty of time to do so behind bars.

Living with some suspicion that I rolled has been tough for me, especially knowing how I feel about keeping my mouth shut. I guess I never forgot what Archie told me when I was just a little kid: "Never open your mouth and you'll never get into trouble."

I'll go to my grave swearing that nobody ever went to jail or got convicted because of me. I never walked into a courtroom and testified against anybody. My prison stay could have been shorter, but I wasn't getting out of prison by talking, which is what usually happens when wise guys go to jail. They start out doing a lot of time, but they get real tired of it. That's what the soldier's death is all about: If you can't take it, do the right thing. Don't start talking, die. Just kill yourself.

Recently, a prosecutor told John P. Contini, a trial lawyer and friend of mine, "You know, we had Walter subpoenaed, and he wouldn't go the route. We gave him immunity, and he wouldn't cooperate. He chose to do hard time."

That is what I chose, and it was hard time. Being hunted in prison is tougher than dying a soldier's death, but I wasn't going that route, either. I wasn't talking, and I wasn't dying a soldier's death. Like I said, there were many times I wanted to die, and I tried to kill myself early on, but I figured out how to survive inside, and I never talked. I went away with lots to tell. No doubt about that. I wouldn't have had to do a day of time. Not a day. But I didn't roll.

In November 1977, I took the fourth attempt on my life. I was carrying a tray out of the prison commissary at the East Unit, and a black cook shoved a spoon into my side. He pushed that spoon into me until his hand was up against my skin, and it took one hundred and eighty-two stitches to close that up. He thought he was going to get some respect, some notoriety, some canteen money for hitting me. They're not going to pay some prison inmate for taking me out. Like I said before, a guy in the circle has to do you to collect the price on your head.

Somehow I recovered from that at Lake Butler Reception Medical Center. Also in 1977, Connie served me with divorce papers. More than any attempt on my life, that came closest to killing me.

When "the test" had come, as it is known on the street to this day, to get me to cooperate, I wouldn't do it. I wasn't getting out of prison by talking, but that was the turning point for my marriage. Connie thought I should do everything I could to save the marriage and our family. If it meant taking the witness stand, giving up the world, and taking us into the witness protection program, then that's what I should have done, in her mind. I chose not to do that. In hindsight, maybe I should have.

I moved on from Lake Butler to Dade Correctional Institution before ending up at Lawtey Correctional Institution outside of Jacksonville, Florida. Four years after going in, the Florida legislature passed the point system. That meant that first-time offenders were given parole dates if they had served fifty-three months or more. In since 1975, I was set to be paroled on February 12, 1980. My father had been released after serving two and a half years of his sentence in Lexington.

CHAPTER TWENTY-ONE

"We're all criminals until we come to God."
—Pastor Wil Cohron

With my first parole set for February 12, 1980, work release was scheduled in Jacksonville, Florida, six months prior. That would be my first time on the other side of the walls since 1975, and I had plans to put my team together right away. I had met a guy named Pete Floyd in prison, and he says, "I'll be your driver."

"All right, you can be my driver," I told him, which was convenient because he was released before me.

So Pete picked me up from prison, and I called Dale and said, "I'm out. Come on up to Jacksonville." Then a week later, somebody sent me $25,000 and a new 1980 Lincoln, powder blue. It was a gift for keeping my mouth shut behind bars, and that's how I got started again.

Both Dale and Marshall were out on parole and we all got trashed our first night together. We went to a strip bar, we're celebrating, and I saw a girl—gorgeous big green eyes—and I gave her $500 for dancing for me. "I'll have to take you to dinner," I told her.

"Oh, I don't date customers," she says. But I got her phone number, and naturally I kept calling her.

The day after I met her, though, I said to the guys at breakfast, "We gotta get our team together." So I'm on the road to start robbing again back in Lauderdale, and the first night we hit $65,000. That was a good score, so I went back to Jacksonville, and I called the stripper again. Finally, she agreed to meet me for breakfast. Her name was Marianne, and we started dating. When she asked me what I did for a living, I told her, "Well, I've got a unique business, that's all." She never thought I was legit; she knew I did something I shouldn't be doing. She just didn't know what.

Before too long, I rented a townhouse on the oceanfront in Jacksonville for $1,500 a month, which was big money back then. Because I wanted to be near Marianne, I brought my team into the immediate area, and we started banging out there. We were doing pretty well, and I was spending lots of money, so Marianne and I got involved.

Besides being a dancer, she was making a lot of money as a call girl. Marianne was thirty-eight, and I was thirty-three, but that five-year difference wasn't important. She was getting ready to quit the dancing business, though, which was going to impact her income.

I said, "You don't need any money. I got plenty of money." I knew I was in good shape, and I was planning to stay in good shape. Finally, I told her who I was and why I was in prison. That didn't seem to bother her.

When I think about Marianne now, I remember loving the challenge of getting her out of stripping and prostituting herself. I thought I was going to save her from her horrible life. Her first husband got her into that life. I was thinking I could bring her around, and that was a mistake. I guess that sounds outrageous, you know, as if I wasn't living a horrible life. I just didn't see it back then.

Naturally, when I told my mom that I had met a girl—a stripper and a call girl—she didn't like it. That was understandable, but when she met Marianne, knowing what she was, my mom says to her, "If you didn't have big breasts, he wouldn't even look at you." That was her harsh tongue again, but she was looking out for me. My poor mother was always looking out for me.

Marianne was from Alabama, and she had two teenage daughters from a previous marriage. We all started traveling together while I was working, and my mom didn't like that either. Like I said, my mother had stayed close to where I was incarcerated, and I was living with her and my dad when I first got out. My dad was out of prison by then, too, and he was back living in

Jacksonville. That was before I rented the oceanfront condo. My parents had high hopes that I would go straight when I was released. Obviously, they were disappointed.

When my mom kept badgering me about living with Marianne, telling me I was setting a poor example for my son and all, I asked her, "Will you feel better if I marry her?"

"No! Don't marry her for me," she says. "Just don't live with her."

"What church do you go to up here, Mother?" I asked her.

"First Baptist Church," she answered. So I went to see Pastor Homer G. Lindsay Jr.

"I want to marry this girl I met, and I need to know if you'll do that for us," I asked him.

He says, "Are you born again?"

"What do you mean 'born again'?" I ask him.

"I can't marry you unless you're born again," he tells me. So I went to the Catholic Church, and they wanted to do the priest thing.

Then I remembered Larry Boardman, a guy who led the prison Bible study. He lived in Jacksonville, so I called him up. The nicest guy in the world, Larry had often come to see me in jail. He was a three-time middleweight champion of the world, and he was also a solid citizen.

"Larry," I said, "this is Walter. I'm out of prison."

"How long you been out, Walt?"

"Two months now."

He asks me, "Why'd you wait so long to call me?"

So Larry comes to see me, and he was just a sweet, sweet soul. I told him, "I want to marry this girl, but I can't find a church that will marry us."

"Well, the church I go to will marry you, but you've got to come to our service first."

"I don't want to go to a service," I tell him.

"You have to come to a service, Walter," he answered.

I had never listened to anything Larry was saying when he came to see me in prison. He'd lead a Bible study, and I'd come by and say, "Okay, yeah, everybody gets saved in prison." It was all jailhouse religion to me. Why weren't they Christians on the street? Why do they have to come to prison to find God? Was God missing on the street?

I hear people say it all the time, "I got saved." Saved from what? "I found God." Was he lost? I hate that expression. Seeing things the way I see them now, I was the one who was lost; God wasn't lost.

Anyway, I wasn't seeing things that way back in the late 1970s. I'd seen a lot of guys in jail get saved. As a matter of fact, I saw John Spenkelink get saved, and I even had his Bible at one time. Spenkelink escaped from a California correctional camp and murdered a hitchhiker while traveling in the Midwest in 1973. After the death penalty was reinstated in 1976, he was the first murderer executed in Florida, and the second in the United States. He witnessed to me in the visiting area one time.

After the Episcopal priest gave him Communion, John gave him his secret epitaph: "Man is what he chooses to be. He chooses that for himself." His last words made a lot of sense to me: "Capital punishment: Them without the capital get the punishment." He must have hated the rich, too. When they killed him at the Florida State Penitentiary in 1979, they were sending 2,250 volts of electricity through a committed Christian. John was the real deal. They flipped the red switch for the first surge; then two more followed that.

Anyway, I go to Larry, and my mom, my dad, Marianne and I are having this powwow about the church thing. Marianne and I decided to go to Larry's service, and we took my kids, Randy and Shelly, and her kids, too. I remember that Marianne and her two girls were smoking grass in the bathroom before we left. They were looking for the courage to darken the door that day. We all piled into my Lincoln, and off we went.

We drove down to a place called Druid Street, which is in the poorest, dirtiest part of Jacksonville. It's right next to a junkyard, and I said to Larry, "They got a church in this neighborhood?"

"Don't you think God needs to reach poor people, Walt?"

"This is your thing, Larry. This ain't my thing." So we pull up, and I park. I'm worrying the whole time about my new Lincoln getting robbed in this dingy neighborhood. I made sure I was wearing my guns, too. I wasn't going back to jail for anybody, so I carried them everywhere with me. I'm not saying I would kill the police before I'd go back to jail. I'm saying that I didn't know who else could be out there. Without them, I felt naked.

Larry says, "Walt, do you feel you need those?"

"It's just the way I live my life, Larry. It's what I am. I'm not a saint."

So we all file in, and this place was blasting music with tambourines, drums and horns. The whole building was shaking. "This is a church, Larry?" I had never heard a church making that kind of noise. The churches I had been to with my aunts and uncles were Catholic. They were quiet and somber, and you dipped your hand in water and all that nonsense.

Anyhow, I didn't want to go in, and I said, "Larry, I'm not going in this place."

He asks me, "You want to get married?"

I said, "Yeah, I want to get married," so we went in. Larry leads us all the way down to the front of the church. The place probably held 2,200 people. It was packed—black, white, orange, green—every denomination, poor, rich, whatever. So we go down, and the whole platform is filled with musicians. There's a podium up there, and there was an organist. She was a gorgeous woman all dressed in black up to her neck and down to her ankles. But she looked different—no makeup, no jewelry. I checked all this out.

There we sat, Larry, Marianne, the kids and me, and I asked, "Is this some kind of joke? This is right out of a movie. What are they trying to be here 'la-la land' or something?"

"Just relax," he tells me.

"So where's the priest?"

"We call them pastors here, Walter," I'm told.

"Where is he?"

Larry tells me he's the guy playing the saxophone, and I'm wondering about a guy who can marry me if he's playing the saxophone. So I watch him, and he puts down the horn and starts talking.

Pastor Cohron must have been about forty-two years old at the time. Very solid, very robust. I later learned that he was one of the fastest collegiate runners in history. He steps up, he leans forward and with a very sweet, calm, Pensacola Southern voice, he says, "Well, I thought I had my sermon all pointed out to me, but God told me to change my topic."

I'm thinking, *Does God talk to you much while you're playing your saxophone?*

"God has instructed me to change my sermon and preach on the life of King Solomon from the Book of Ecclesiastes," he announces. I didn't know the meaning of the word and couldn't pronounce it at that point.

He goes on, "You know who Solomon is, congregation? Solomon was the richest man of his time. He had more women, more liquor, more gold and more silver than any man alive, or any man that would come in the future." That got my attention. I gotta get to know this Solomon guy. I didn't know there were people like that in the Bible.

I'm nudging Marianne saying, "Yeah? So how'd he get it? This guy's got all the gold and jewelry in the world. So how'd he get it?" I decided to listen to this.

Pastor Cohron's sermon was penned for me. Unbelievably, though, he didn't know who I was at the time. Larry hadn't said a word to him about bringing a jewel thief to church with him that Sunday. He didn't know anything about Walter Shaw, and he preached a two-hour sermon to me that morning. The guy held me. He spoke from the spirit; he spoke in tongues. Even for a guy like me, it was moving.

The message was so good, in fact, that Marianne was crying next to me. The call girl was crying tears. I'm looking at her, and she says, "Don't you feel that?"

"Feel what?" I remember asking her.

"That they're speaking to us, Walt. This message is for us."

I tell her, "No, I don't feel that."

When Pastor Cohron gave what is known as an altar call, she put her hand out to Larry. He was going to take her up there, and I tried to stop them. "Walt," please don't do this. If she wants to kneel at the altar and be prayed for let her go," Larry told me.

"Please, Walt," she says, looking at me with those big green eyes, "I need to be prayed for, and you do, too, but you won't listen. I know where I come from. I know the life I've lived."

So she goes up, and I said, *All right, I'm going to watch this charade. It's all bullshit.*

Marianne goes up there, and these other women gather around her. Like the organist, they're wearing long, weird dresses with their hair piled on top of their heads—no makeup. I'm watching this like some kind of cartoon. They lay hands on her, and she starts sobbing some more. All of a sudden, her hands go up like there's a stickup.

As a matter of fact, when we walked in the door of that church, they were all holding their hands up in the air. It looked to me like they were all being robbed. Larry had said, "Walt, they're not being robbed, they're praising God. That's how we praise God here." It scared me just to see it. It looked like they were all getting arrested to me.

Anyhow, my girlfriend's hands go up, and Pastor Cohron comes down, gathers everyone around her, and he lays his hand on her head. Now she's accepting Christ into her life, knowing she's a sinner living with a sinner. They're whispering, but I can hear it. He says, "There's another thing we do here, and that's a baptism. We want you to be baptized with Christ. Do you want to do that?" asked the pastor.

And Marianne says, "Yes."

"Where do they do that?" I asked Larry. Just about that moment, they roll back a platform, and there's a pool in there, a baptismal. I had never seen a pool inside a church before.

"She's going to be baptized in there," Larry tells me.

So Marianne comes out of the back wearing a white gown, Pastor Cohron's in rubber boots with suspenders, and a lot of men and women were lined up to get baptized. She's the sixth one in. They go down and say a bunch of words, and I can't hear them then. I'm up there in the front row trying to listen to all the babble.

So that I could be nearer, Larry moves me around closer to the baptismal. I'm watching while Pastor Cohron is holding her and saying things to her. Then she comes out of the water, and it kind of worried me. She shoots up soaking wet, and she looked radiant. It was the most mind-blowing thing I'd seen in my whole life. Marianne was still crying, and then, all of a sudden she's speaking in tongues. She says something like, "Allah shamnay…" I'll never forget that moment as long as I live.

Backing off the podium I was reaching for my guns again. Larry asked, "What are you reaching for, Walt?"

"I don't know what this is, Larry, I mean, it's scary."

"It's God, Walt. Stay out of it."

At that point, I'm petrified, and I had to talk to her. I know this girl. I've gotta talk to her. Her hair's all wet, and she comes out to me with a big smile and all glowing, and I said, "Marianne, what was that about?"

"I got married to him," she tells me.

"You got what?"

"I'm married to God," she answered.

We were sitting down, and I said, "You're married to God?"

"And there's another thing," she tells me, "God told me I can't marry you until you have what I have."

"Hold it right here. I'll be right back." I'm steaming mad, and I run over to the pastor.

Larry steps up saying, "Walt, please, what are you doing?"

"I want to see this guy, this pastor, whatever you call this phony. Get him over here." So he does, and I said, "Friend, we have a problem."

"What is that?" he asked sweetly.

"I came here to get married. Larry said your intentions were to marry us. My name is Walter Shaw, this is my girlfriend, and we live together. Now, let me tell you something, I've heard about charlatans; I've heard about churches; I've heard about scams; I've heard about all kinds of crap. I don't care about any of it, but whatever this gibberish, this bullshit…"

"Be careful about poking fun at God," he warned me.

"I'm not careful about nothing. I don't fear man. I don't fear nobody. This girl tells me we can't get married until I have what she has, and I'm not going to have what she has because I am a criminal."

He said, "We're all criminals until we come to God."

"This ain't real," I told him. "I'm going to follow you. I'm going to dog you, and if this is a phony, you don't have to worry about any more of this crap. I'm going to send you to meet your God."

"Okay, that sounds good," he told me, and didn't blink an eye.

I didn't even have to show him my guns. I told him I'd send him to see his God and never think twice about it, and he says, "Okay."

We were all staying at my mother's house at the time, and I didn't know then that I had walking pneumonia. I got real sick that night with a raging fever. A few days go by, and because she's married to God now, Marianne and I are sleeping in separate bedrooms. She was wearing dresses down to her ankles, going to church every night, wearing no makeup, no jewelry, got the hair on top, and she's carrying a big Bible everywhere. I wasn't getting involved with any of it.

This went on for a week, and I was sick as a dog. I had stuff stashed in Marianne's safe deposit box, and I had to get it out and sell it. It was two weeks that I had been down with pneumonia. When I asked her to go get it, she told me, "Walt, I don't have it anymore."

"What the hell is that supposed to mean?"

"I gave it to the church," she announced to me.

"You gave $70,000 in jewelry to the church. Are you crazy?! My men are going to be up here wanting their end."

"Well, I gave it to the church."

So I get dressed, and I go see Pastor Cohron. "Listen, this girl put some stuff in the offering, and I need it back."

He said, "Well, I saw jewelry in the offering, and we got rid of it."

"You gotta get it back," I told him.

"That money belongs to the Lord, Walter."

"Is that so? Has God been robbing people's houses lately?" I went out of there irate. Fit to be tied, I did some real bad things to his house and his cars. Cohron was getting the message that way.

Marianne and I separated over that. I was miserable, and my team was working farther south again. The guys thought I'd lost my mind. Out on a job with Dale, I dropped a pry bar on a patio.

He said, "Walt, what is wrong with you? You never dropped a pry bar in all the years we worked together. You're making first-timers' mistakes out here. You'll get us killed. Go back to Jacksonville and get yourself together." So I went back.

I moved into a motel room up there, and I'd just made $50,000. Drinking Jack Daniels, I was trying to drown my sorrows. I thought about shooting myself I was so miserable. I had some money, but I'm drunk, depressed, my mother's mad at me, my dad's ashamed—I mean, just nothing was working.

It came to me to go down to the church, which I did. I walked in there, I walked up to Cohron, and I spit in his face.

"How's that grab you?" I asked him.

"Walt, do you think that means anything to me?"

"Yeah," I tell him.

"What else do you want to do? Do you want to kill me? Do you want to knock me down? Whatever you want to do, do it," he said.

"Why is that?" I asked him.

"Because Jesus in me loves you. No matter what you do to me, I love you. If it's not Wil Cohron who loves you, it is Jesus Christ who loves you."

I can remember saying, "You're an amazing human being. I don't know where you get that from." And I left. I had never encountered anything like that. Next to what I did to my dad, though, more than anything else in my life, I regret what I did to that man that night, spitting in his face like that.

Before Thanksgiving in November, I walked back in there, and I laid my guns down at the altar. I looked at the Pensacola pastor, he came down and embraced me, and he said, "You remember one thing: You come to God the way you are, in the garbage can that you are in, and God will do the rest. If you think you're going to come to God when you're straight and cleaned up, it's not going to happen. You'll never come to him. If you knew me the way God knew me, you'd never get saved."

"What do you mean?" I asked him.

"That's the way it is, Walt. Do you think I've been perfect all my life? You come to God the way you are, and God will do the rest."

That night I told Pastor Cohron all the rotten, wicked things I had done. I also told him that I needed something bigger than guns and the Mafia and all the rest of it. He laid hands on me, and he said the sinner's prayer: "Ask Jesus Christ to forgive you. Tell Him that you know you are lost and undone and that you are a sinner. You don't have to name the sins, He knows them. Just tell Him that you need Him."

"Walt," Cohron said, "life isn't going to go away for you. It is going to follow you the rest of your days. What you've reaped, you're going to sow. It's scriptural, but God will do the rest now. Now you have to do something to help yourself. You have to figure out where you go from here."

Very soon thereafter, Marianne and I got married by a justice of the peace.

Pastor Wil Cohron and his wife, Shirley.

CHAPTER TWENTY-TWO

"Man is what he chooses to be. He chooses that for himself."
—John Spenkelink, Death Row Inmate

Given all that went down with Pastor Cohron, I committed myself to going straight. Marianne and I were married, and I was reading the Bible and trying to go a new way. My dad and I are both out of prison, and we're talking again. In fact, we had the same parole officer in Jacksonville. That's how strange and sad this story is.

Anyway, I got a job working on a construction crew. I was hired by the Woodbine Naval Station in Woodbine, Georgia, at four bucks an hour. That was the first time since working at Schiff's Shoe Store in 1968 that I went looking for a legitimate job.

Not surprisingly, though, everything began to fall apart. Marianne and I were at each other's throats. I wasn't making any money, and she was used to money. Ultimately, she went back to dancing, and we separated again.

While I'm still working up in Georgia, I learned that the feds were coming after me with a subpoena to testify against Aniello Dellacroce, underboss of the Gambino crime family. Aniello says, "You gotta go into hiding." So I'm dodging the subpoena, they're out there trying to find me and I went back to Jacksonville.

I found Marianne, and she asked, "Do you want to try again?" By then, I had violated parole by working in Georgia, and I was thinking about returning to robbery. Obviously, I was no longer praying the sinner's prayer.

Marianne had left the fold, too, and she tells me, "Somebody's got to make some money, Walt. I won't go to jail for what I do, so let me try to make some money, and then I'll quit."

"No, you can't do that," I told her.

She says, "I love the Lord, Walt. What happened to me was real, I know it, but what I do won't get us arrested." So she went back to dancing again.

Marianne and I were going to celebrate Christmas together that year, and I remember going out to buy a Christmas tree. The feds were still looking for me. They knew I had been out of town, violating my parole. Marianne thought they'd excuse me for that since I'd been working construction, trying to change my life, and I decided to report my parole violation.

On December 11, 1980, I went down to see my parole officer. I told Marianne to wait for me in the car, and the parole officer says, "I've gotta go to the men's room, just wait here, I'll be right back."

Rather than waiting, I decided to leave. When I was walking down the hallway, I saw two guys step off the elevator. They were walking towards me, and I was walking towards the elevator. They said, "Walter?"

"Feds? My parole officer turned me in, didn't he?" I asked.

"He's violated you," they told me, and they took me downstairs to a holding cell. Marianne comes in crying, and she's telling me she'll wait for me.

"No, you won't wait," I told her. I was being transferred to Tallahassee Federal Prison. I had been out for nine months, and a lot had happened during that time. If I was violated, I was going back for a lot of time; I wasn't going back for a day. Even though it was a technical, I could go back for ten years.

When Marianne came to see me, I told her to let me go. "They're going to transfer me to Butner Federal Penitentiary in Durham, North Carolina. You gotta let me go."

She says, "I'm not going to do that, Walter."

And I said, "Do it."

When she was leaving, she said, "I met a gangster in a bar once."

And I said, "Yeah, I met a lady in a bar once," and she left. We used to say that all the time, but that would be all over.

So I'm sent to North Carolina, and I was reading the Bible in the visiting area, trying to figure out my life. I got a call one night, and it was the pastor. I said, "What is it with you?"

Pastor Cohron said, "Walt, I want you to know that of all the people in your life, this Pentecostal preacher will be waiting for you at the gates of hell before he sees you go across."

"You mean that, don't you?"

"If you go back for ten years, I'm going to be there waiting for you."

In North Carolina, I went to trial on a double parole violation—state and federal. That's where I happened to meet John Hinckley, who had shot President Reagan on March 30, 1981. Sick kid. The feds said they were going to turn me over to the state, and ten months later I was back in Lake Butler Medical Reception Center in Florida.

After a week, I got a call from Pastor Cohron again. He says, "I'm coming to your sentencing hearing today."

He had been checking on me, begging for my life. You know, saying, "Please restore him. Don't throw him back in jail." I don't know why he did that, but that's what he did. They reinstated my parole in August 1981, and I got out again.

Pastor Cohron had been moved to another church by then, and they were building a new one. I literally went there every day to help him build it. I stayed with him and his wife, and I even enrolled in Luther Rice Seminary in Jacksonville. I had quit stealing totally and wasn't doing anything wrong. But that was too tough for me. I wasn't strong enough for the world yet, just wasn't there. The world was still pulling on me.

Unfortunately, I had met a guy named Richard in prison, and he came up from Miami to find me in September 1981. He was in trouble and was running from the law. After posting $47,000 bond by using his mother's house as collateral, he jumped bail. I was still with the pastor at the time, but Richard and I started working together, robbing again. "Gotta leave for a while," I told the pastor.

He says, "Walt, don't do this."

I answered him, "I can't stay here with you and be doing wrong. I just can't do that. I can't sit in church and be out robbing that night or the night before."

"Then don't rob," he told me.

"I have a friend who's in trouble," I told him, and I left. He knew I was in trouble, too.

Even though I was sinning, I still came to Sunday services in that big, beautiful new building. I would put a decent amount of money in the offering plate on Sundays. One time he needed an offering for carpeting in the new building. I had made a big score, and I put six or seven thousand in an envelope that time. I knew the pastor would never take the money from me, so I put it in the plate in his name.

A couple of days later, he called me, and he said, "I found an offering in my name."

"You did?"

"Yeah, just what I needed for the carpet," he tells me. "Walter, did you do that?"

"I can't tell you that."

At the time, I was dating a girl, and Rich was dating a girl. Ironically, the girl I was dating was a Christian. One night she tells me that, and she says, "Walt, I heard you used to be saved once."

"Yeah," I told her.

"I used to be a preacher's wife, and when we got divorced, the world got a hold of me."

And I said, "Well, if you knew 'the way' once, then there'll never be anything between us."

We stayed friends, though, and she went down to Miami with

me. I cashed in packages, and she knew I was back in the life. She couldn't prove it, but she knew I was robbing again. In her mind, she thought that giving Richard up would get me back to Pastor Cohron, which would get her and me together. So she and her girlfriend dropped the dime on him. He was already on escape, a fugitive, and they called the cops and reported a fugitive living at his address.

When the cops raided Richard's apartment on March 18, 1982, I happened to be there, too, on the phone with my dad. He was in Nevada, and I was getting ready to go see him and my mom. I says, "Dad, I gotta call you back." They were at the door to raid the place, and I jumped out the window, but they got Rich.

I was hiding underneath a stairwell outside. Some kids were at the top of the stairs, and the cops were armed. Because of the kids, I came out and gave myself up. I didn't want those two little kids to see that happening. The police knew who they were looking for when they came around. They already had my car, and they had that surrounded.

When we go to jail, Richard confesses to everything. A real fish, he tells them about all the jobs we did, doesn't leave anything out. I will never understand it, but then he decides not to testify. He changed his mind, but the judge wasn't letting me go. He tells me he's going to violate me. "We're not trying you, but we're going to violate you." So they violated me on what I had left, what I owed the state, which was seven to eight years. I was going back to prison in March 1982, for my second parole violation.

The day before I was arrested, I had found Marianne again. I had been looking for her, and her daughter told me where she was. Suffering from cervical cancer, she was retired from the bar. She was doing accounting work. That night, I went to her house to see her. I was all dressed up and driving my 280Z. I had tons of money, and I walked in there feeling good.

She said, "I see you're back in action. For how long?"

"I don't know," I told her. "The hounds are on me. I know they are. I can feel it."

"So, how's Pastor Cohron?" she asked me.

"He's fine," I told her.

She got tears in her eyes and said, "I never went back, Walt."

"I knew you wouldn't."

She says, "It was real. Everything I felt in church that night was real. I will never deny that."

"How about dinner tomorrow night, just for old time's sake?"

"Okay," she says, "pick me up at seven."

"I'll be here."

So I was leaving, and she says, "Walt, did a lady meet a gangster?"

"Yes, she did," I answered. I was arrested the next day.

I called Marianne from jail. She had seen the papers, and I said, "We're not going to make dinner."

"I know that, but I appreciate the call. I guess it's just never been an easy thing for either one of us, has it?"

"No, it hasn't," I told her.

"I hope you get out of it, Walt." That was the last time I talked to Marianne.

Pastor Cohron had opened the door to Christianity for me, but I was on the wrong road again by the time I went back to prison. I guess I was trying to get to prison for a lot of years. The whole time I was involved in criminal activities, I was being schooled for prison. There are only three things that can happen to a criminal: 1) you get away with it for a season, 2) you go to prison for the rest of your life or 3) you get killed.

I remember seeing a sign when I was sent to the East Unit of Florida State Prison. That's where one of Florida's three death row cellblocks and its only execution chamber are located. You'll remember, there was a time I could see "Old Sparky" from my cell. The state sends you to Florida State Prison to get the point across.

As a matter of fact, FSP is Florida's only so-called "prison," the other institutions being called "correctional institutions." Going in to the unit there was a big sign saying, "End of the Line." The next place you're going to is hell. Prison is a shadow of what's to come if you're not right with God. The lights are on all night, and people are screaming and yelling and clanging on the bars. If you can't take that, you're not going to make it in hell, that's for sure.

There was a nineteen-year-old kid assigned to my cell one time. He was a nice-looking boy, just crying his heart out about being sentenced to three years for auto theft. This was after I'd been released and sent back for violating my parole. I was in my ninth year by then, and he was crying, "Oh, I got three years."

I was thirty-something years old, and I wasn't into his whining. I remember saying to him, "What did you think, kid, that it was going to be a picnic? You thought you were going to stand before the judge after you stole the car and say, 'I'm sorry, let's change all this and let me go?' It doesn't work that way. That's not the real world. You break the law, you get caught, you're gonna pay. This is your punishment. I got three years in one bathroom. I don't want to hear about your sentence; I got that in one chow line."

"You must be some kind of hardened criminal," he says to me.

I yelled, "I handcuff lightning, shackle thunder, walk through the graveyard and make the dead wonder. That's what I do."

"Wow, you really are a bad guy!"

"I am a bad guy," I told him. He was scared to death of me.

I shouldn't have screamed at the kid, but I had done a lot of time and still had a lot of time facing me. I'm in my thirties. My twenties are over. Reality was setting in for me, and I didn't want to hear about a kid with three years. But if you got a day, a hundred days, or a hundred years, time is time. Prison time is lost time. I hate it that my youth was wasted, thrown away.

I'd like to think I could talk a group of kids out of getting into the crime business. Because of my past, I think I can talk with some authority, at least about organized crime. There are kids out there who might think this life sounds exciting. Hollywood tries to make the mob appealing, but it ain't Hollywood, and it ain't *The Sopranos*. Go out to a graveyard and dig a hole sometime. See how appealing that is. Watch somebody get shot three times and draw his last breath. See how appealing that is. Trunks of cars—walk around with that for a while. People are only enamored with the intrigue of the mob because they haven't walked that walk. It's one thing to see a war movie; it's another thing to fight a war. Go into the trenches, watch somebody's guts spill out on the ground, and see how you feel then. There is no happy ending in a life of crime. There are no successful criminals, not one. They may be successful for a season, but you'll never meet a successful criminal. Criminals make it to prison or the grave. One is hell on earth. Where you spend eternity is a choice you make.

Just recently, I watched an eighty-one-year-old guy, an underboss of the Gambino crime family, get convicted and sentenced to life in prison. Where's the success in that? He's asking for mercy, and the judge says, "Did you give mercy to the victims you extorted and killed?" If you want mercy in this life, you have to be merciful. There are only two places you can go as a criminal, prison or the grave.

The first eighteen months of my second term were spent in Avon Park Correctional Institution in Avon Park, Florida. Three times a week, Pastor Cohron made the trip there from Jacksonville. It was only because of his dedication that I was transferred to Lawtey Correctional Institution near Jacksonville. The pastor visited me every day when I got there in 1983.

CHAPTER TWENTY-THREE

"Every sinner's got a future, and every saint's got a past."
—John P. Contini, Criminal Defense Attorney

After my dad got out of federal prison in Lexington, Kentucky, and before I went back in, I did one of the worst things I've ever done in my life. I hate admitting this. I introduced him to a guy named Al in Jacksonville. Al was a fence of mine, and I thought he had some money—money that could do something to help my parents financially. Somehow in the course of their meeting one another, Al talked my dad into making the boxes for money again. He had said, "Listen, I can sell some of these. Just make a few of them for me."

My dad's an ex-convict by now. Of course, the prison system had seen the benefit of having him incarcerated while serving his time in Kentucky. He had overhauled the entire phone system at the Federal Correctional Institution in Lexington during his two-and-a-half-year stay there. He's out again. He's an electronics genius, a penniless inventor, and he got involved with Al to take care of him and my mother. They were going out to Reno, Nevada, after that. Like I mentioned already, I was talking to him out there when the cops came knocking on Richard's door in Jacksonville.

Shortly after that, things went bad for my dad again. Turns out, when Al was reeling my father in to make the black boxes, he was out on a drug charge, which nobody knew at the time. The authorities had knowledge that he was around my father, and when things were all set up for Al to go to prison, he started talking. My mom and dad are living in Reno by then, and my dad gets busted. Just trying to start over out there, his arrest was so upsetting he had a heart attack. He recovered, but he went to jail in Nevada.

Now we're both in jail again, and I've got no money to bond him out. The case against him is in Jacksonville, and I call Pastor Cohron from Lawtey for some moral support. Unbelievably, and without my knowing it, Pastor Cohron, who had never met my dad, put up his house or his boat, one of the two, and bonded my father out.

"Why do you do these things?" I ask him.

He says, "I have watched what God has done in your life, and I believe in you, Walt."

When my father comes to Florida to make his appearance for the arraignment, Pastor Cohron picks him up. He drives him down to see me, and I'm in shock. It was the first time I had seen my dad since going in the second time, and he says, "Listen, Thiel, whatever is going to be is going to be. Don't worry about me. I'm going to be okay." He's trying to tell me not to be thinking about some kind of revenge against Al.

"Are you sure?" I ask him.

"I'm sure," he tells me.

My father's case went to trial, and the judge gives him probation. This was probably in 1984, and my poor mother was elated. "It's a miracle. God let him get probation," she's telling me. That's just the way she talked. But he had to make restitution. That was part of his deal, and they came back to Miami from Reno.

About the time I was incarcerated at Lawtey, the prison system started a new four-year educational program there called Zoe Bible College. Christian professors were coming in to teach classes for those of us who wanted to sign up. Even though it was faith-based, because I had never done anything in the way of higher education, I felt a need to educate myself. That's the reason I signed up for the course, and Pastor Cohron was all for it, too.

Knowing what I know now, to my way of thinking, the King James Bible is the greatest book ever written, and nobody wants to read it. It isn't a stretch to say that I was fascinated by the Bible, and I wanted to learn more about the scriptures. I remember reading a book written by a guy named Freddie Gage. He was an evangelist preacher who worked with youth gangs. Gage wrote the same thing in all the Bibles he gave to people: "The Bible will keep you from sin, and sin will keep you from the Bible."

When I first met John Contini, a man of faith, he said to me, "Every sinner's got a future, and every saint's got a past." That's a great quote, and it's the truth. We are all sinners. Even murder is not the unpardonable sin. The unpardonable sin is the rejection and denial that Jesus Christ died on the cross and arose on the third day. That's the unpardonable sin. That's what sends you to hell, and you send yourself there. I have led a horrible life, but I have finally come to those principles.

I don't want to beat anybody up with my Christian beliefs here. I'm not thinking that my book is going to make anyone turn to the Lord. I know it's not. Most people won't accept the idea of me being a Christian anyway. I was a thief, and nobody believes a bad guy. My belief is just my personal thing, and it's the only road for me. That doesn't mean it's the right road for you, but it's the right road for me. And I'm not saying that I haven't fallen from grace, come back and fallen again. I have, many times. I'm just sharing this here because it's important to my story.

I had talked to Pastor Cohron about my plans to attend Zoe, and I can remember saying to him, "You know, I don't want to be just another parishioner." In my life, it doesn't work to know a little of this and a little of that. I wanted to go all the way with God. Just like thieving, I put my whole heart into it. I know that sounds ridiculous, like thieving and Bible study have something in common, but I put my whole heart into everything I do in my life.

Of course, I had second thoughts about what I was doing at Lawtey. I had met a girl during my time there. Her brother was going to get beat up pretty bad in prison, and I saved him. Because of that favor, he introduced me to his sister, Joanie. She got on my visiting list and came around five nights a week. Joanie was gorgeous, a real knockout.

When I got involved with Joanie, I was thinking about quitting school. She was planning to get a real estate license in California, and she wanted me to head that direction when I got out. Joanie knew I was into the whole Bible thing. She was Greek, wasn't into what I was learning, and I was going to quit school over that.

She had said, "I'm not going to be the way you are, Walt."

I thought about it. I talked to Pastor Cohron and others about it, and the lights came on. I had come so far in prison, how could I go back?

So I called Joanie, and I said, "I've decided that you will probably be going to California without me."

Looking back on it, that was one of those things you call a chain gang romance. They happen all the time. When you're isolated, you meet different kinds of people from the kind you might meet on the outside. There is something about marrying a guy in prison. A woman feels safe. She feels in control of the relationship. You know, she doesn't have to make a real commitment. Mentally, she might be committed, but that's it.

I met another girl when I was in prison. We had a four-year friendship, and she got caught up in the evangelist thing with me. I was going to spend my time doing revivals when I got out in April 1986. That was my plan, and Gloria was going to be singing in them for me. I had graduated from Zoe in December 1985.

I did exactly what I had planned to do, and my first revival was with Dr. E.J. Daniels, who is right up there with Billy Graham in my view. Everybody knows him in the Baptist Convention. He was a tent revival preacher, and his platform was old school: fire and brimstone. Get 'em saved; get 'em to the altar. He discovered me through Senator Dan Jenkins, who represented the 7th District in the Florida Senate. I was out on work release from Lawtey, and Senator Jenkins liked the evangelism work I was doing. He invited me to an election rally in Jacksonville, and later introduced me to his minister, Dr. Harold F. Hunter, who comes out of the Southern Baptist Convention in Jacksonville. Dr. Hunter saw some promise in me, too.

Anyway, a staunch, crusty, old Southern Baptist minister, E.J. Daniels liked me. When we first met, he said, "You're God's trophy, and God can take you from the gutter most to the utter most. That's what I see in you if you stay the course." That was in 1985 or 1986.

After I got out of prison in 1986, I preached to some of the biggest drifters in America, all across the country. I had singers with me, and we were doing all kinds of revivals. I didn't do those for any set amount of money. I wasn't interested in that. I would do it for an offering. When I was beginning to get a name for it, I remember a guy coming to me in a Church of God camp meeting. He says, "I'm kind of ashamed to ask you this, you being so big now, but I have a little church in Bradenton, Florida, and I'm wondering if you would come and witness to us? We only have thirty-five people. I guess you wouldn't come for thirty-five people."

"I'm not that big," I told him.

"Well, I can't afford to pay you," he said.

"Can you feed me?"

"Yeah, what do you like to eat?" he asked me.

"Black-eyed peas and grits. That's where I started in life."

The pastor said, "Sure, I'll feed you."

So I went to that little church and true to his word there were thirty-five people in attendance. In those days, I split my preaching into two services. I ended the first service with my arrival on Death Row. Then I said, "Now you've got to come back tonight to hear the rest of the story."

Sharing my testimony at a Bill Glass Crusade in 1987.

Speaking at Lawtey Correctional Facility in December 1986.

The pastor and his wife had four kids, and he came to me after the first service, and he says to me, "Walter, would you mind eating in your van? My wife's kind of worried about this." She's figuring I killed somebody.

"Did I scare her?" I asked him.

He says, "Well, she's a little worried."

More people showed up that night, and I tell the congregation that I wasn't on Death Row to be executed. I was there for protective custody. The pastor's wife comes up crying to me at the end, and she says, "I am so sorry."

"Why are you sorry?" I asked her.

"Because I judged you," she admitted.

"Hey," I tell her, "I understand why you were scared, but we're all on Death Row. Until we're saved that's where we're at. You don't have to kill anybody to get there."

When I got out in 1986, I met my third wife, Barbara, at a revival. She came to hear me preach, and Gloria saw what was happening. I recall her saying, "Walt, she's coming to you out of a divorce. It's not going to work. It's got all the warning signs."

Being hard headed and stubborn, I married Barbara. That lasted ten months, a disaster. Barbara and I were getting involved with Jim Bakker's ministry, and we were going to go up to North Carolina. I had gone to Jacksonville and been ordained and licensed with the Church of God, and I was going to be in the prison ministry. In the middle of all that, though, Jimmy falls, and Barbara goes nuts. "This is all phony crap. I don't want any part of this. I'm leaving you," she tells me.

The world thinks that guys like Jimmy Swaggart and Jim Bakker are crooks. You can be a messenger and a great evangelist; it doesn't mean you're going there yourself. They are just men; they aren't Christ. Christ is the example, and He uses people to get the message out. Because they were still called of God, I've never ridiculed either one of those men.

There's a line from *A Few Good Men* that I love. Kiefer Sutherland says, "And God was watching." It's true. God is watching. He doesn't miss a beat. Whatever we do, whatever we think we got away with on this side of life, it's going to be unveiled on the other side, every bit of it. God knows where I'm at.

I had gone to see Pastor Cohron after I got out of jail the second time. When I saw him, I said, "You know what, Pastor? I'm confused. God used a hooker in my life, and she left the fold."

He answered me saying, "Walt, God uses many things in our life to reach us, and He allows many things to sway us. Marianne had the same opportunity that you have had. We don't know why she didn't stay, but you did. God allowed her to be the instrument to bring you into my church. Otherwise, you never would have come. That was your time, Walt, it wasn't hers. It was your time, and God used her to get you there."

My time didn't last long. Within a matter of months, my third marriage ended, I lost my mother, the most important person in my life, and I would disappoint Pastor Cohron again.

CHAPTER TWENTY-FOUR

"You sound like a guy telling me he's got the cops around the corner."
—Crystal Shaw

I haven't written anything about my younger sister, Crystal, but she figures into the rest of this story. I'm not out to hurt anybody here. Keeping it real, though, some tough things happened to my parents because of her. My mistakes where my parents were concerned were no less hurtful, and like I said at the outset, life doesn't keep secrets. It is what it is.

Nine years younger than me, Crystal was the apple of my dad's eye. I'll admit to resenting that. My dad really adored her, and I believe he was hoping she could be what I was never going to be. Maybe she wouldn't go down the crooked road.

My little sister started playing the piano at five years of age, and she excelled at that. No doubt about it, she had talent. Palm Beach College gave her a scholarship for singing a cappella, which is Italian for "in the style of the chapel"—whatever that means. But that's how much potential she had. Even more amazing was the fact that she could sing in four languages. My mother and dad even hired an Italian opera singer to give her voice lessons. They had high hopes for Crystal.

You're wondering how they paid for that. Our mother was working switchboard to pay for all of that. Every dollar she made went to Crystal. Whatever my mother had to do to make some money, she was doing it. They paid for a Steinway on credit, and we were eating eggs and Wheatina. Crystal always came first. Me being the big brother, I had to take care of my little sister. The spoiled brat that she was, I'll admit to resenting that. I used to call her a spoiled little bitch and I'd get chastised for that. I loved her because she was cute. I did love her for that, but then she went and dated a wise guy.

Crystal dated Sam Caputo's nephew when she was sixteen, and my dad came and told me about it. The kid was married, and I went to him and kindly said, "You're married. This is my sister, my dad's daughter. Don't do this. I'm giving you one warning."

He says to me, "You know, Sam Caputo's my uncle."

So he's declaring himself to a level, warning me to think twice before I did anything to hurt him. That didn't matter to me; I tracked them down to a hotel, and I caught them there together. I never gave my dad the details, but I grabbed her, threw her in the car and went inside and pistol whipped him. Broke the kid's jaw.

Once again, he declares, "You know who I am, don't you?"

I tell him, "I don't care who you are. I'll go to the sit-down, and I'll answer for it."

Lo and behold, after I gave him the beating, Donaldson and I had to go to the sit-down at Sneaky Pete's. I'll never forget it. I'm at the table with the guy that represented me. I wasn't on that level with Sam. Sam was a major guy. But I went in there with one of Anthony's men, and he says, "Now, don't speak, just sit there and listen and say *yes* or *no*. Don't get crazy. We may not leave here if you get nuts. This guy's a major player."

So I sat there, and Sam says, "Hey, you, did my nephew declare himself?"

"Yeah," I told him.

"And he did this before this happened, isn't this correct? And then when it happened, he still declared himself?"

I said, "Let me tell you something. He told me before, he told me during and he told me after, and I told him I didn't care. That's my sister he's with, and he's married."

My guy next to me was going nuts. He's nudging me under the table, and Donaldson was on the other side. You know, as if to say, "You're getting up in this guy's face when we're here for a sit-down?" They didn't care, and they knew I didn't care.

Caputo said, "Who do you think you're talking to?"

"It doesn't matter who I'm talking to," I told him, "you know the rule about family."

"That's why you're walking out of here. Don't ever think about crossing the street in front of me again. This is the only pass you're going to get from me," he says. "Crossing the street" means coming around him or in front of him or in back of him.

When I got back to Crystal, I said, "Now it's over with. Don't hurt Dad again if you can help it."

After that, Crystal was with a guy named Russell. So they go out to Vegas together, and Crystal lands a job opening for Ann Margaret. Then she opened for KC and the Sunshine Band. She even opened for Frankie Valli, the lead singer for the Four Seasons. I called all the favors I could because of her voice. Even Wayne Cochran wanted her. She was that good.

Russell was a good kid, a legitimate carpet installer, a hard-working stiff, just a nice guy. They had one child out of wedlock, and my mother went out there when the baby was born. Then they had another kid after they were married. My mother knew Crystal wasn't mature enough to be having children. She wasn't responsible, and my mother was big on helping when the grand-children were born.

After Elvis had overdosed and died, Crystal was in Vegas with Wayne Cochran doing an Elvis tribute. That's when she and my mom get into it. She didn't like my mother telling her how to take care of her kids. She actually hit my mom and knocked her down the stairs, which broke my mother's arm. Crystal even locked her out of the house, and my mother had to go to a hotel. It was really bad, but my mother was too afraid to tell me the truth about that.

I was in prison by that time, and she came to see me with Crystal soon after that. When I saw the cast on her arm, I asked her, "Mother, what's the cast about?"

"Oh, well, Crystal and I got into a big fight. You know how I am. I yelled at her about the kids and she didn't like it. She locked the door in my face, it was icy, and I slid."

I'm not buying it, and when Crystal went out to get something from the car, I asked my mother again. That's when she told me the truth about the stairs and all.

I'm livid now, and I tell my mom, "Crystal better make sure I never get out of jail."

When Crystal came back in, I jumped up from the table in the visiting area of the prison, and I was yelling and screaming. She sees me in my tirade, and I says, "How did you think you were getting away with this?"

"You're in prison," she tells me, all haughty.

"I am? What does that mean?" I ask her.

"You sound like a guy telling me he's got the cops around the corner. Do you think I care?"

I says, "You know, I don't care about God, children, cops or anything, I'll crack you where you're at." Not even God was getting in the way of that.

"No, you won't," she said, and I jumped up from the table and swatted her. I chased her across the yard, and, of course, they came out and locked me up. They put me in the hole, in fact. My mother was crying and carrying on, and after that I told her never to bring Crystal back to see me.

She said, "Oh, Thiel, please. She's lost. She's a sinner. She needs our prayers." My mom made a million excuses for her, and she was probably right.

While I was locked up, I told Crystal over the phone one time, "Let me tell you something: When she dies, you're going with her, so just realize that." I don't think I meant it, but I said it. "You're going down right next to her." That had pushed me over the edge. She locked our mother out of her house.

Vegas cancelled Crystal's contract because of her arrogance. She may have been a good singer, but she was no "prima donna." They finally got rid of her. Even Frankie Valli and Wayne Cochran chased her away. She was so good she even had guys writing music for her, but Johnny Masters, her bandleader and arranger, gave up on her, too.

"I can't deal with your sister," he told me. "She's a nightmare. She won't come in on time, she doesn't hear her cues, and there are too many other people who can make it with less talent than her." Crystal wasted her life.

The week my mother was dying, I remember her crying. She knew she was sick, but she didn't know how sick she really was. We didn't tell her that she had leukemia. When the doctor gave us the diagnosis, my dad and I just looked at him. We didn't know what leukemia was. Never heard of it. We knew it was a real bad disease, but we thought there was a cure. Then this oncologist says, "There's no cure."

Anyway, my mother was holding my hand one day—we all took shifts, never left her alone at Mt. Sinai Hospital where I had her in a private room—and she says, "Thiel, I want your word. Whatever happens, even if I get out of here, I want your word that you will look after Crystal. Pray for her, but don't hurt her. This is a family that loves each other. Remember that."

I said, "Mother, don't worry about it." I meant it, and she died that Sunday, Mother's Day, May 11, 1986. I'd been out of prison since April.

CHAPTER TWENTY-FIVE

"Fifty-one years wasn't long enough, Betty Lou."
—Walter L. Shaw

Losing my mother was the hardest thing I've ever had to deal with. It was just as traumatic for me as losing my dad ten years later, maybe more. Though I may not have shown it, they were the two most important people in my life. I'm saying that, but I couldn't stand to be around them because of what I was. They knew where I'd been.

Just before I lost my mom, I was getting ready to preach a sermon in Alabama, and my dad called. I had never heard him cry on the phone before, and he says, "Your mom's real sick, Thiel. Please come home."

I dropped what I was doing and drove all night to get there. When I made it to the Howard Johnson's on Miami Beach, I cleaned up first—shaved fresh, nice cologne—and I ran into her hospital room to see her. I said, "Mother, if you wanted to see me, you didn't have to do this, go to this extreme, you know," trying to keep it light.

While leading a prison ministry banquet the following week, I got the call that she was dying. When I heard that I was frantic about getting Pastor Cohron on the phone. I reached him at a revival in North Carolina to tell him my mother was dying, and he asked, "How long?"

"Days," I told him.

"I'll be right there," he said.

"But you just started a revival."

"I'll be right there. My friend needs me." Pastor Cohron arrived within hours of my mom's death, and she knew he was with her.

My dad had gone to get Crystal at the airport, and my mother died before he got back. Because of his heart trouble, I was standing watch at the elevator to try and shield him. They called a "code blue" and worked on her for an hour and a half, but they lost her anyway. My older sister, Linda, a nurse, came out to tell me our mom had died.

When my dad came in, he bent over and kissed her. I saw that from the corner of the room. The way the light was shining on him, it was the first time I ever saw my father as an old man. I'll never forget it, he said, "Fifty-one years wasn't long enough, Betty Lou."

Crystal had come into the room with him, and she was leaning over my mother trying to wake her up, trying to tell her she was sorry. I was still standing in the corner when Crystal looked up at me. Fear grabbed her and she says, "Thiel…"

I said, "No worries. I promised Mother I'd never touch you. We'll never speak in this life again, but I'll never touch you. The next time you want to tell her you're sorry, you'll have to be in heaven to do it."

Pastor Cohron stayed to do her service. Standing up there he said, "This woman exemplified God's love. She loved her son at his worst, and that's how God loves us."

At the end, I asked him, "Where do you get this stuff?"

"We're all loved at our worst by God, Walt. He doesn't love us at our best; he loves us where I found you, in the garbage can. Think about what I told you back then." He had told me to come to the Lord as the garbage can I was and that God would do the rest.

So we had a big funeral for my mother, and we buried her in a crypt. My dad hadn't wanted her to go in the ground. She was afraid of going in the ground. I found out a few days later that he had buried her with bad checks. He was staying with me then, and the guy called me and said, "We're going to have to move your mother. The checks bounced."

I told him, "Don't touch her. I'll take care of it." So I went to a wise guy for the money.

"What do you need, Walt?" he asked me. He gave me what we needed. He knew I was good for it. Until I went down and paid them, though, they wouldn't put the plate on.

I wasn't mad at my dad for doing that. That's just the way he was. He didn't have any money, he didn't know what to do, and that was the story of their life together. My mother would follow him from eviction to eviction, hoping that the next invention would get them to their pot of gold. I saw everything my parents went through together. It was a tough life, but they loved each other.

After she died, my dad wouldn't go back into their apartment. He had Linda and me go in. He says, "I can't go back in there." So my sister and I go in, and our mother had four dresses hanging up in the closet. Four dresses. It was so tough smelling her perfume and just picturing her in there.

I was real distraught after my mom died. I remember going to see Pastor Cohron. Just sitting there in his house, I said, "I can't do this anymore, Pastor. I can't live through this. I just can't do it, I'm telling you."

"Yes, you can," he told me.

"No, I can't do this anymore. I can't live like this. That was my whole life, my mother. I never got to do anything good for her. She died with four dresses in her closet." I couldn't get those four dresses out of my head. When I left I told him how much he had meant to me, that I loved him and knew he'd been my friend.

I had some Valium with me and six cans of beer in my car. Sitting in his driveway around nine o'clock at night, I took the pills. It seemed like there were about a hundred of them, and I washed them down with the beer. I don't even remember going through the red light that night, but that's what happened, and I drove off the road. When the cops found me they saw the pill bottle and the empty beer cans. They had me. I was arrested for that, and I woke up in the hospital at the county jail.

Standing before the judge, I told him I'd just lost my mother. He says to me, "I know. I'm sorry for your loss, and I'm not going to hold you. I'm going to release you on your own recognizance. You were beat up bad enough, and I'll see you on your court date."

When I returned to court, I didn't get probation. I got a fine and driver's school, and the humiliation of that was rough, but surprisingly, the judge had shown me some mercy. In all honesty, I've received more mercy than I've given.

Barbara left me after that. We hadn't slept together since my mother had died. I slept on the couch. Wasn't functioning. I was done.

I'd been preaching at revivals before my mother's death, "Satan wants the world to look good to you, but don't live down to the world's standards." And I would always quote one of my favorite scriptures, Matthew 7:14: "Because straight is the gate and narrow is the way which leadeth unto life, and few be there that find it."

I couldn't do it. I couldn't live up to God's standards. I lost my way again, gave up evangelism, went back to robbing people, and my dad moved to Reno to get away from the memories. He said to me, "We're not helping each other, Thiel. You're in misery, and I'm in misery, and I don't know if you'll ever come out of this one. I've gotta be with your little sister." Crystal was a drug addict by then, and he wanted to take care of her and her kids. It was years before I found out that my dad was supporting her with his Social Security checks.

The last portrait taken of my parents, 1985.

CHAPTER TWENTY-SIX

"Your dad isn't like the other guys."
—Lieutenant Cox, Assistant Warden, Lawtey Correctional Institution

When my mother died in 1986, my dad quit paying his probation fees, quit reporting. Didn't care anymore. He just gave up on life and violated his probation. Nothing was important to him after losing my mother. He made a few trips back from Reno during that time, and on one of those trips he had another heart attack. My sister called me from the hospital to say he'd had open heart surgery. Of course, I ran right down there to see him.

Somebody had told on him, and by the time I got down there they had him surrounded and handcuffed to the bed. Literally, he had just come out of surgery, and within a few hours they had him in cuffs. Who could do that to an old man? When he saw me, my dad waved me off, and the marshals said, "If you go near him, we'll arrest you." I went ballistic and the cops grabbed me.

My dad's laying there on oxygen, and he asks us to stop. "Don't go back to jail over this, Thiel." This was at Holy Cross Hospital in Fort Lauderdale in 1988.

I can remember saying, "If you weren't cops... You know..."

"We know, and that's too bad, but we're wearing a badge, which means we can get away with it," they told me.

After that my father goes to jail up at Lawtey on a violation. I had gotten out about two years earlier in 1986, and Lieutenant Cox, the assistant warden, called me. He says, "Walter, your father's here, but we put him on the outside detail so he'd be in the trustees' dormitory. He's working on the compound during the day, doing a new phone system for us."

Lieutenant Cox had recognized my father's name and asked him, "Do you have a son?"

My dad says, "Yes, he was here, too."

Cox said, "Yeah, he came in here as a tough guy and went out with a Bible."

So Cox did me that favor for my father, keeping him out of the prison population. I remember saying, "I appreciate that, Lieutenant."

He says, "Well, your dad isn't like the other guys." Lieutenant Cox was also the one who laid down the law that my mother wasn't to be searched when she came to visit me. He knew how good she was.

One of the most tragic things about my dad's story was going to prison so late in his life, and all over not paying probation fees. He didn't care anymore. He had lost my mother, and nothing else mattered.

By the time he got out in 1990, I was back robbing people, and he was back in South Florida for a time. He was consulting with a female doctor, and she calls me up and says, "Do you have a father by the same name?"

"Yeah, I do," I tell her.

"Well, I just operated on a man by the name of Walter Shaw, and I had to remove his testicles. He's at the Beaches Hospital here in Fort Lauderdale."

I drove over there, and sure enough, it was my father. I remember saying to him, "How long you been here?"

"A couple of days," he tells me.

"Why didn't you call me?" I ask him.

"Well, you know, I didn't want to bother you."

"You know that's not the reason, Dad, but how long you in town for?" I said.

"Not long," he answered, "but they found cancer." That was right after he got out of Lawtey. They had detected it there, but he didn't tell me that. He wasn't going to have the operation up there.

"Can we go to dinner when you get out?" I ask him.

"Yeah. When I get out, come back and see me," he says.

I came back the next day, and he was gone. He left. Went back to Reno to be with Crystal. So I asked the doctor what he had, and she tells me he had prostate cancer. "How long does he have?"

"Well, we removed the testicles to slow the disease. That could buy him five or six years, but eventually the cancer will kill him."

CHAPTER TWENTY-SEVEN

"There's no such thing as one more score."
—Walter T. Shaw

In 1990, I closed out with Dale, quit stealing. I couldn't keep the pace. He came back for me one night, and that's when I said to him, "This is my last job. I'll get you killed or caught if I keep doing this." That experience with Dale turned me. My dad hadn't died yet, and I looked at Dale and said, "I can't cut it."

Dale says, "I learned from you. I can't leave you, Walt."

"Go with my blessing and earn," I told him. "You don't need me anymore. You have surpassed me."

He had surpassed me. Dale could do more and bigger scores and get away with it, but like I said, there are no successful criminals out there. Dale's in prison now.

One time I was interviewed by a reporter about Dale, and he said, "Walter, you got all misty about him."

I said, "Yeah, because I led him down a road that I wish I hadn't. I'll always regret that. He wasn't a bad kid, but now he's not a kid anymore. Only fifteen or sixteen when he came with me, Dale never really had a life, and now he has nowhere to go."

The reporter said, "You're taking the blame for that?"

"Yeah, I am," I told him.

I'm also taking the blame for what I did to my son. I was passing out cigars and drinking with my friends when Randy was born. Connie had just delivered him, and I was late getting to the hospital. I remember her saying, "Even for this you couldn't be here? What was more important than the birth of your son?" That was July 12, 1969.

My son, Randy, is probably the most generous, compassionate kid I know, but he wanted to be a thief like me. There was no doubt in my mind, though, that he didn't have the heart for it. When he was learning the business years and years ago he wanted to go on a caper with me. I wanted to make sure he knew what he was doing—didn't want to see him get killed—so we went out together. I know I shouldn't have done that, but I did it anyway. That was all it took to know that Randy didn't have it, and that's why I told him to give it up.

He's not a tough guy, and I said, "You know what will get you killed in this business? Having too much heart will get you killed doing this. That's why you don't belong in it, Randy. You've got too much heart to be a criminal, and not enough the other way to do it the right way."

I did what I could to keep my son out of stealing. One time we had an especially heated confrontation over it. He was drunk and high on coke, and he came around yelling and pointing his finger at me. It was one of the few times I ever had to hit him. Just out of jail, I'm renting a place for $1,500 a month, I've got a new Lincoln, and he screams, "You've got all this! I want what you have!" (He's telling me he wants what I got, and when I was my son's age, I wanted everything my dad never got.)

"What have I got?" I asked him. "I got a rented place. I got no friends I can trust. I got a rented girl I change every night like underwear, and whatever else I got is in my pocket. Is that what you want? That's what you think I got?"

"Well, you've got a reputation," he says.

"What is that going to do for me? I've gotta be watching my reputation for some young kid trying to take it from me. What've I got?"

He's looking at me, listening, and I tell him, "You're looking for superficial stuff, Randy. You'd trade any kind of solid relationship for a prostitute or a woman that's in it for the name? That's what you want? In this business you don't even have to do something wrong to get whacked. They're going to kill you because they thought you did wrong. You want to take a chance like that with your life? Isn't your life worth more than that?"

He says, "Dad, I just want to get one more score. I want the big one."

"There's no such thing as one more score," I told him. "You'll be going back to that life if you go for one more score. I'm telling you there's no such thing as one more score." I used to live on that promise. It never happened. I just couldn't run fast enough anymore.

Randy and Shelly lived with my parents during the first year I was in prison. My father had watched the same thing happening all over again with his grandson. He saw Randy going the same direction I had headed. My son, though, was never the criminal that I was. Unlike me, he's never hurt anybody. He's not that kind of kid.

Randy wept his heart out when my father died. That was really tough on him. He was late for the funeral and asked them to open the casket so he could kiss his grandfather. I think he thought he'd lost the best part of his life. We both lost the best part of our lives. His bond was with my dad, not me. I had that same opportunity with my dad, and I blew it. I went the full gamut, trading my soul for the Devil for a season.

You pass a time in the world where I come from when you can't go back, when you've crossed the line as my dad called it. There was no going back for me. I was either going to die in the rackets or I was going to prison forever. That was it. There was no going back. I knew too much, and I was too great a threat to a lot of people. They weren't letting me out. When you're a wise guy, you don't just say, "I quit."

My father wouldn't cross the line, though. He wouldn't go farther than the boxes. We both went down this road, but when we came to the fork, we separated. He turned right and got away from the rackets, and I turned left and pursued them. If I had it to do all over again, I'd go right with him. I chose the wrong direction. I know that.

The biggest mistake in my life was the loss of my relationships with my parents, my first wife and my children. I can't replace them. I have four grandchildren, and I've only seen them once. I don't see my two kids anymore either. There's a price, and you're going to pay the price if you choose this life.

When my daughter was sixteen, she came to prison to see me. I remember her saying, "Daddy, will you ever change?"

And I said to her, "There's no reverses, Shelly. I can't go back and apologize. I've already committed so much crime." I was thirty-five years old then.

In 1990, though, I reached the point that I didn't care anymore. I retired from jewel thieving after that last score with Dale, and I haven't been involved in stealing anything since. Of course, I'm not denying that the rackets didn't tempt me, but when I lost my father in 1996, there was no question in my mind. I remember saying, "I'm never going back out there. If you want to kill me because of what you're worried about, you'll be doing me a favor." I really didn't care what they did to me. Nobody in life could do any more to me than I had done to my dad. My mind was made up. I was done with the rackets under any condition. I was finished.

Do I wish my dad had never met a guy named Archie? I've asked myself that question a thousand times. "Truth day" came around in 1973. A year later, I ran into Tony, (the guy who had moved in with my mom, my sisters and me when my dad was in New York making the boxes), at a 7-Eleven on my way home one night. I'll never forget it. I says, "Hey, Tony, what brings you south?"

He tells me, "I'm here with my dad. He's got the restaurant, and I came down here to work with him. By the way, did you hear that Archie died?"

"No, I didn't," I told him.

"Yeah, he died last week, and we're all going up for the funeral. Are you going?"

No," I told Tony, "I'm not going up."

"Why, not?" he asked me.

"Because he finally told me the truth about the black box," I said.

So I didn't go to Archie's funeral in 1974. He had broken my heart, and I was no longer that eleven-year-old kid who'd met him at the Grand Concourse Hotel. I still had the walk he'd have recognized anywhere, but I'd lost all my innocence. We all lose our innocence, but I lost mine hurting others to get what I wanted. It took me fifty-eight years to get to the Magic Kingdom in Orlando, Florida, and I didn't want to leave. I hadn't seen innocence since I was a little kid. I've had to lie and cheat most of my life to stay alive.

CHAPTER TWENTY-EIGHT

"Why wear jewelry? I know who I am."
—Frank Sinatra

The world had its way with me for a long time. When I was at the height of my career, I used to say, "I steal to live, and I live to steal." In my early days of robbing people, it was all about the money. If I couldn't be a rich boy, I would find a way to be a rich man. I was going to be a real blueblood.

I have spent a lifetime justifying my criminal behavior by what I saw done to my father, but I also went down this road because I don't like doing poverty. Poverty was the result of his situation, and I don't like living broke. Like I tell everybody out here, if you're broke and you're just surviving, you're also in prison; you just don't recognize it. That is my philosophy. It's my line. You're in jail because you can't go out and spend money.

Why didn't I get a job somewhere and climb the ladder? There was a time I thought I might want to be a trial lawyer, but that was going to take eight years. That was too long to wait for the lifestyle I wanted for my children. I didn't want them to have one pair of shoes. If I wanted to give them fifty pairs of shoes, that's what I wanted to give to my kids.

One year, I rented an entire amusement park for my son and his friends. It was a place on 163rd Street, and I rented the whole park for his birthday party. That cost me $5,000, and I couldn't have done that on a waiter's job. It would have taken too long to afford that legitimately. My kid would be ten years old by that time, if even then. I also thought I would be giving my mom and dad things they never had, but they never took anything I had to offer. Except for that El Dorado they thought I'd gotten legitimately, they wouldn't accept anything from me.

Money to me was all about spending it. I used to fly to Maine three times a week for lobster, and back then it cost me $500 a trip. One day at the racetrack I blew $150,000 on a single horse. That's what money was all about to me. I couldn't put it in the bank. Connie had a checking account under an alias and her name, but we had to have phony IDs and all that nonsense. Except for the money orders to pay the rent, everything in my world was paid for in cash, and safe deposit boxes were the only way to keep it. Rather than dealing with the money, it was simpler just to spend it.

So I dressed the part in my fancy clothes. Like a showman, I was wearing the latest fashions from Vegas. I wore all kinds of different colored suits and brought as much attention to myself as I could. In fact, when the cops raided my house on the search warrants, the authorities found 110 suits in my closet. And I had forty pairs of shoes to go with my 110 suits! I know that because they counted them. One of the newspaper articles I kept says, "Fancy dress and fast talk, Walter Shaw finally goes to jail." You know, I lived the life back then.

It wasn't until I got older and understood what was happening around me that I changed my spending habits. Years ago, Meyer Lansky told me, "You're going to wear one suit at a time, drive one car at a time and live in one house at a time." This was a guy worth $300,000,000, and he drove a 1967 Chevy Impala. "You don't have to spend money to prove anything. You want to keep them off, not draw attention."

And Anthony said to me, "You're banging on that wall, kid."

"What do you mean, I'm banging on that wall?" I asked him.

He says, "Looking for attention is banging on the wall. You're being flamboyant in your big houses, big cars and fancy clothes, and you got no job. What do you think, they're stupid? They're just sitting back letting you do what you want? You're banging on the wall, and the police are on the other side. You're going to crash through to the other side if you don't stop. They put a guy in prison named Al Capone because of what you're doing, Thiel. He's been where you're trying to go." Anthony's philosophy was sound.

You might ask how I could go to prison, get released and go right back to stealing that night. When I went to jail the first time, a Cadillac was nine grand and a Lincoln was eight all tricked out. The average cost of a new home was $40,000, and gas was forty-four cents a gallon. Everything changed by the time I got out in 1980. What was I going to do? Was I going to give up living because of the threat of jail, or was I going to have a life again? My choice was to have a life again. I went back to my old team. They couldn't believe it. They said, "What, you're ready to go again?"

I told them, "Yeah, I'm ready to go again. Let's go knock the doors down." And we did. I took down another couple million dollars in that short spree after I got out in 1980. We did another hundred homes in Jacksonville alone. That was in the eight months I was out after my first term in prison.

So how could I take the risk of going to prison again? Did I have a fear of prison before I went to prison? I was risking it before; why wouldn't I risk it again? Prison isn't a deterrent. Prison doesn't change anybody. It's a warehouse. It holds you. If I wanted to be able to afford a life of some kind, I wasn't going to let the threat of jail stop me. Every night I went out to rob people, I knew there was the potential for me to lose my freedom. I was willing to take that risk.

So it's not about the threat of jail. I was robbing until the day I went to jail. In fact, I was working the night before I went to court to pick my jury in 1975. I was out on bond, and that night I took off a score in Las Olas—bagged another $150,000. I told my wife, "If something happens to me, you know where it's at." Jail's never been a threat to me.

But I switched gears at a certain point in my life. I toned it down. Instead of going for a $3,000 custom made suit, I'd wear a $500 suit off the rack. I didn't need to drive a flashy car, either. The first go-round I came out and bought a 280Z, and I paid cash for it. I definitely switched gears. It was time to practice what the old masters were telling me through the years, and that was especially so when I was closing in on fifty.

Would I like having money again? Sure. If I had all the money I could possibly want would I be happy? No. I've been there. More money would make it easier to pay the bills, yeah. I liked living without the pressure of figuring out how to pay for things, but when you get older and see what's really going on, you change. I look at things totally differently now. I don't need forty pairs of Italian shoes to be happy. In that respect, I've grown much more like my dad in my later years. I don't need a lot; I just want to be able to make it.

I met Frank Sinatra when I was a kid, nineteen or twenty. I was just breaking out in the rackets. Tony Plate, a wise guy who is now deceased, used to have Sinatra appear at the Diplomat Hotel in Hallandale. Whenever he came, we'd get comp tickets to be in the front row and center, and Tony introduced him to me. There's a saying, "He's a friend of ours, you know." In other words, he's with us, without saying it. So Tony would introduce us and say, "He's a friend of ours," and Sinatra knew what that meant.

I said to Sinatra one time, "You don't wear much jewelry."

He says to me, "Why wear jewelry? I know who I am."

I guess you get there as you mature. You know who you are without the clothes and all the other stuff. What do they say? The clothes don't make the man; the man makes the clothes. It's the same thing with jewelry.

When I got out of prison the last time, one of the cops took me on as his personal challenge. He says to me, "We're going to make you like the Florida panther."

"What's that supposed to mean?" I asked him. It may be Florida's state animal, but I was never paying much attention in social studies.

"There is an animal in Florida called the Florida panther," he told me. "Mankind is making it extinct, and that's what we're going to do to you."

So I took that on as my trademark—license tag, jewelry, my wife's jewelry—everything was a panther. I even made up Christmas cards with the Florida panther. I signed one for that cop, "From the Panther." It was a joke. I used to wear a heavy gold chain with a black cat medallion and a yellow-gold pry bar hanging on it. You know, it was all about the whole cat burglar thing. Yeah, it represents what others see as unlawful. In the underworld, though, no other profession was more romanticized than being a cat burglar, and I've already admitted to being proud among my peers. But I don't wear it anymore.

I stole a lot of beautiful stuff, but I never kept it. Possession of stolen property, that one beautiful piece, could send you away for fifteen years. That's how I looked at it. There was nothing that valuable to me, and I could always make a duplicate, or go out and buy my own beautiful pieces. That reminds me of a stroke of luck I had with Salerno in New York. We had a fence on Park Avenue—used to make Liz Taylor's jewelry—and Pete and I were shopping for watches. As it happened, an heir to the Firestone fortune was in there wearing a top hat and overcoat buying a 23-carat marquis diamond ring for his girlfriend. Listening in to the conversation, we learned that his new ring was to arrive by truck at his home back in Boca Raton, but I'm not admitting to anything here.

Harvey Firestone, Henry Ford, and Thomas Edison are considered to be three of the greatest inventors and corporate leaders of their time. All three spent their winters in South Florida, and all three were part of a very exclusive group called The Millionaires' Club. My dad came along years after them, but he should have been one of them. Instead, he got nothing for what he invented, and he was sweating it out in South Florida year-round.

When I see a diamond ring in a window, just to stay sharp, I still do the game of guessing what carat weight it is. If diamonds hadn't been an allure for me I probably wouldn't be sitting here writing this story, but I don't feel that way anymore. Diamonds have only taken from my life; they haven't added to my life. I feel the same way about all my dad's inventions.

CHAPTER TWENTY-NINE

"I have always said that people should be proud of what they do."
—Oprah Winfrey

ack in 1970, a New York City Police Department detective contacted me. He wasn't looking to accuse me of anything. Eddie Egan, whose exploits were the subject of a book and movie, both entitled *The French Connection*, says to me, "I'd like to do a movie about your life, Walter. I'm putting a production company together in Florida." Eddie's company was Gold Shield Productions, and I thought the whole idea was a goof. I wasn't ready then, but he told me to call him when the time was right. "Give me a shot at it," is what he said, and we became friends.

I looked Eddie up when I got out of prison, and we put something else together. I was trying to do something legitimate, and he made an instructional video for me intended to educate viewers on how to protect their homes from burglary. Eddie is featured in the video, and it was actually the last thing he ever did. It came out in 1990, and we called it, *It Took a Thief to Stop a Thief.*

Years later, Alan Greenspan's wife, Andrea Mitchell, got burglarized for several million dollars, and she is a friend of Oprah Winfrey's. She says to her, "One of the most notorious jewel thieves in the country, Walter Shaw, is out of prison in Florida, and I think you should call him. He's made a tape about preventing robberies."

The next thing I know a woman by the name of Kim calls me from Oprah's show. I thought she was pulling my leg at first, but she says, "We'd like to have you on the show."

I said, "Is this a joke?"

"No," she tells me, "we really want you on the show." Then she tells me they want to tape the show in my own backyard. "You pick out the houses, and we'll film you breaking in," I'm told.

I know a lot of influential people in South Florida (there was a time when I was studying all of them in *Forbes*, *Fortune*, and *Who's Who in America*), and we picked out several to film. They also wanted me to travel to New York. The technical advisor on Jodie Foster's movie *The Panic Room* asked me to come up to do a house after he hardened it. "Hardening" means putting in an alarm system. He was going to make the place burglar proof, but I broke into it in thirty seconds. He wasn't thinking with a criminal's mind.

As recently as July 26, 2007, Detective Brian Burdick from the Los Angeles Police Department called me about the Hillside Burglaries out there. A skilled burglary crew has been targeting some of L.A.'s wealthiest neighborhoods, and he was looking for some expertise in trying to catch them. I guess that might prove my point that it takes a thief to catch a thief.

I have never met a house that I couldn't break into, but I'm not looking, either. There's always a weak spot in a security system, which reminds me of my dad's favorite saying, "If I can draw it, I can make it." I can say with some assurance that "if man made it, man can break it." There's no alarm system that can't be broken.

I did Oprah's show in 2003, and she saved me up there. Though I was her guest, the audience was grilling me pretty hard. One lady in the audience really wanted to lay into me. Oprah had warned me that I had to face the music with my appearance. I assured her I could do that, and she said, "Please be gentle in your responses, Walter."

"I will," I told her. I knew what she meant.

Anyway, that particular lady said, "You know, I have a hard time with you being on here, knowing who you are. My house was robbed, and it wasn't very nice. I think you're the wrong person for us to listen to."

Oprah says, "I believe he should be listened to because he's been out there."

"Well, I think it's a disgrace to have him on your show."

Oprah asked me to comment on that, and I said to the lady, "I can bet money I didn't rob your house." That's all I said to the lady, betting on the fact that she wasn't in the same league with the Fortune 500. Oprah knew exactly what I meant.

As it turned out, she had a lot of mail over that appearance. Not that she was saying I should be excused for my past behavior, but she stood up for me. She says, "Listen, Walter is not here to be abused. He came at my invitation, and he was gracious enough to do so. I've interviewed murderers and rapists on this show, too, and until I've walked in their shoes, I'm not going to judge them. That's all I have to say about the subject."

So my appearance on *Oprah* was a result of the tape Eddie Egan shot for me. Looking back on that show, I remember telling the audience that our gang was sometimes called the "Cartier of jewel thieves" by the FBI. I see the crack in myself for saying that. You know, I'm on there trying to be a legitimate guy, but I'm telling stories like I'm some kind of hero. I'm sounding like Pete or Don up there. I regret that.

In that special way she has with humor, Oprah says, "I've always said that people should be proud of what they do." Then she asked me a question: "Do you feel bad?"

I remember telling her, "Yeah, I feel bad, and I will give back my half if they give back their half." The audience is wondering what I mean by that, and I told them, "They double claimed me. If I'm the guy who stole it, I should know what a piece is worth. They were claiming a million-dollar loss on a $500,000 piece of jewelry." You know, the rich think they got a license to steal, even from insurance companies. What I should have said was, "Do they feel bad about robbing my dad?" I want to know if the rich feel bad about robbing my dad. I want to give it right back to them.

CHAPTER THIRTY

"Thou Shalt Not Steal"
—God

"Do you feel bad?" Oprah's question is just one of the things I get asked. "Did you see what you were doing as being wrong?" That's the number one thing people ask me. The answer is, "At the time, no." I wasn't looking at what I was doing like that. I saw it as an easier and quicker way to make the money bigger. I made a moral choice—immorality, but I didn't see it as wrong. Like I said before, I was out doing what I was doing because I don't like doing poverty, and I justified my actions by what I'd seen done to my dad.

I remember my sweet mother saying, "Don't you care what people think about you, Thiel? They can think badly of you, or they can think good of you. Don't you care where the money comes from? People know where it's coming from."

I said, "Mother, when you go through the line at A&P to buy milk, do they ask you where you got the money or do they take the money and give you the milk? I never saw a name or a label on money, but it's all got blood on it." That's what I told her. "All money has blood on it. It was made through stocks and bonds, or it was made through gambling; but you won't see any labels on it." So that's how I answered that, and that's how I saw it. It didn't matter to me where the money was coming from.

During the McClellan Senate Subcommittee Hearings in 1963, Joe Valachi said something to the committee that explains my feelings on the matter: "Well," he said, "after you get used to burglarizing or committing crimes, you don't think these things are crimes. I don't know how to explain it. I had dress shops. I had horses. Everyone was selling stamps. How am I going to explain it to you, senator?"

Valachi was right. After you do hundreds of burglaries they all run together. Burglary doesn't seem like a crime, it feels like a job. And it doesn't matter how many you've committed. What mattered was seeing my two children when I got home safely. Knowing I was going to have Christmas for them, knowing they would never have the childhood I knew—that's what mattered. Stealing was about what it was going to do for my family and me, and how we were going to live and have the lifestyle that was not afforded to me as a kid—at any cost. It all goes back to cost: What are you willing to sacrifice to get what you want?

I was raised with the Ten Commandments and the Golden Rule. My parents tried to teach me that things were black or white, right or wrong, and good or evil, but that didn't interest me. I didn't see what I was doing as wrong; I saw it as a way to make money quickly. And I was taking from a society that had taken from my family. While we were doing poverty the corporate guys were getting richer.

There are men and women in this country worth billions of dollars. They could solve a lot of ills with that. But they'd rather buy another Lear jet than go down to Liberty City in Miami and feed the hungry. Oprah's the exception to that. There should be no impoverished people in our country. We feed other countries, but we've got homeless people at home. As bad as I have been, I have never refused a poor person on the street. That doesn't make me a hero, but I have always given when I can. I don't care if they wash cars or stand on street corners; I'm not going to judge their hearts. They can be faking it until they make it, but I'm going to give them something. That's the way I believe.

Do I regret that I stole a lot of jewelry from the rich? I regret that I could have been Robin Hood, but I wasn't. I was young, I was angry and I was spending it. If I were out there now, I'd be doing differently. Helping the poor could be the one clean spot in my life. Just like Valachi said, "How am I going to explain it to you?" I was a bad guy, and I was as dark as all the things you dislike in me. You should dislike me for what I was doing. You couldn't be a nice legitimate citizen if you didn't feel that way about me.

Am I asking for society to forgive me? I'm not looking for society to forgive me; not at all. People will never forgive me for all the wrong that I've done. I've been on *Larry King,* the "king of talk," with this story, and no matter what I have to say, man will never forgive me. Once a criminal always a criminal. No matter what I do, nobody will trust me. I will never get that. Until I am blue in the face and the cows come home, I could scream from the Eiffel Tower that I'm sorry, but it's not going to make any difference. Nobody cares if I'm sorry. That's what I've sacrificed. I will never be trusted.

"Thou shalt not steal" is one of the fundamental Ten Commandments. Whether it was jewelry or the rackets, I was stealing something from somewhere. But I am not sorry about stealing jewelry, not in the sense you might think. I am sorry about the life I've made for myself by taking the jewelry, but I'm not sorry about taking the jewelry. I can't go back and change it, though. Nobody can change the things they've done in their life. I know I went the wrong way. Knowing what I know today, I would never live my life over the same way. I've been a thief and a criminal. My whole life is one of regret.

I'm a recovering thief, and one more score would be turning me back in the wrong direction. I'll be held accountable for one more score, and God's the only one who can forgive me. I'm not looking for mankind's forgiveness.

It's been very hard to stay straight all these years. I beg, I borrow and I struggle every day to stay straight. When my wife's father died, my sister, Linda, sent her a condolence card. She wrote in there that she thanked God for her. "You've kept my brother straight all these years," she wrote. "I don't know where he'd be if you weren't in his life." My wife, Diana, has been the reason that I've kept the gun out of my life. I'd probably be back in prison without her.

CHAPTER THIRTY-ONE

"It's big men playing little boys' games."
—Diana Shaw

I met Diana through the wife of a friend of mine, a wise guy, in January 1993. Diana was going through her third divorce at the time. After fifteen years of dating then marriage to a man who preferred the clubs, she didn't want to raise her kids that way. Diana walked out on money when she left him, but she's never been impressed by money. Having lots of stuff doesn't interest Diana.

Anyway, we're both at a place called September's, and we meet, shake hands, and I thought she was attractive, but that was it. Around that same time, I was going through the end of a brutal relationship, and my mind's all twisted—a real mess. To get my head out of that, I bought a house to refurbish on Bayview Drive in Fort Lauderdale. I'd been working six weeks remodeling that house, doing all the labor myself—the painting, scraping the doors, the whole nine yards. One night I said to myself, *I'm giving myself a break. I'm going out tonight.* So I went out, walked back into September's, and there's Diana.

She's divorced by now, and I'm out of my relationship, so we struck up a conversation. "What are you doing?" she asked me. I told her I was remodeling a house, and she says, "You're crazy."

"Come on, I'll show it to you," I tell her.

So she goes with me to my house, the lights are all on, and she sees that I've got all the rooms torn apart. I was really doing what I told her I was doing. When I asked if she'd like to have dinner some time, she gives me her card and says, "Call me at work."

"I'll call you tomorrow," I tell her.

I'll never forget it. She says, "If you say you're going to call me, call me, you know."

Like I told her, I called her the next day, and we had dinner and a few drinks, which I never do, and the next time we go out, she brings her girlfriend along. That didn't matter to me; she was a friend. She knew who I was. Everyone around Fort Lauderdale knows my name.

As the story goes, I'd been looking for a guy who owed my partner some money, and I spotted his car at Rino's. I made a U-turn to head back, and I told Diana and her girlfriend, "I've got to go inside for a minute." So I go in to see this guy, and he gets up and puts his kid in front of him.

I says, "Carlo, don't do that. I don't want to throw you through the window with your kid in your arms. Put the kid down." So he puts his kid down, and I throw him through the window. He'd been cashing checks at the bingo hall, and I was the one who'd allowed it. The last check was bad, which made me look bad, and I told him I'd be back for the money the next day. Carlo owed my partner $6,000 by then.

Now, I had told the Italian guy who owned the place, "Don't have this guy come in here if you don't want any problems. If I catch him in your place, I'm going to hold court." I'm talking about my court, the court of the street.

When he saw me coming through the door that night, he'd said, "Please, Walt." I reminded him he'd been told he'd have to suffer the consequences if he let Carlo into his place, and I warned him to get out of the way.

It was a principle thing with me. Carlo was told that he owed the money. He knew he wrote bad checks at the bingo hall, and he knew I was looking for him. He disrespected me and still spent a couple of thousand dollars a week in Rino's. If he could do that, he could pay the bill. Like I told the owner of the place, I had also told Carlo we were going to hold court if I caught him again.

I remember saying to him, "Carlo, you can't beat the people that gave you credit at the bingo hall then bang checks out and not pay the bill. It comes back on me. I approved you. Now, when I find you, we're going to have a problem."

You only hold a sit-down if a guy is connected. Carlo wasn't connected. He was a wealthy Venezuelan, an alcoholic going through his father's inheritance. This was different. When you have a sit-down, you've got a beef with another family member, and you've got to iron it out before you take action. That was not the case with Carlo. I was sending him the message that the next time around it would be worse than going through the window. Of course, he pays me the next day.

So Diana's standing outside my car that night, and she and her girlfriend see this guy come flying through the window. She didn't run away at that. She told her friend that they should get in the car and wait for me. Diana knew she had nothing to fear from me. I was just taking care of business.

That was our second date, and I said to her, "Bet you haven't had a date like this before."

She says, "I knew who you were, I just didn't know that every-thing they say about you is true." You know, you can read things and hear things about a guy, but if he looks normal, it doesn't seem true.

Like she told me, Diana was aware of my past going in. Through her law office she ran a check on me with the FBI. She wanted to know if I was really all those things she'd heard about, and her research turned up all those things. I don't do that anymore, though, passing out threats and all. But I'm not in the business anymore, either. Most of the guys who go around passing out threats are trying to prove something, and there's nothing to prove.

Diana and I still pop in to September's once in a while. One evening a while back, it was real quiet, but off in the corner was a guy who just got out of jail. He was one of Nick Guido's guys, and he was starting to get loud. As soon as somebody starts talking loud, you know they want to get noticed.

The owner of the place says, "Can you go over and talk to him, Walt?"

"Sure," I tell him.

"You don't have any bad blood with him, do you?"

"No bad blood. I'll handle it."

So I went over there, and he says, "Who are you with, kid?"

At this point, I'm no kid. It had been twenty years since I had seen him. He had gained weight, I had gained weight, and we're looking old now.

"I'm still with Anthony," I told him, and the guy went ballistic. I thought he was going to bite me in the face. "If Anthony was here, you wouldn't be saying that," I said.

The owner says to me, "What's wrong with you, Walt? I asked you to go over there and be nice."

When I first met Diana, I was still doing quite a bit of yelling and screaming and story trading, but things have changed. A lot of things in my life have changed since meeting Diana. We were just friends in the beginning, and we talk about that. Neither of us thought it would go anywhere. In fact, she tells me she never thought I would be attracted to her. She figured I'd be looking for a blonde with big breasts, the typical wise guy's girlfriend. Diana's not a wise guy's girl. I fell in love with her because she's Marilyn Monroe on the inside. I got the most beautiful woman I could find. Most of the wise guys' girls are nothing but dead bones inside.

When we were six years into our relationship, I was in Los Angeles on one of my trips about my movie, which is a subject I'll be getting to. Diana got serious one night on the phone, and she says, "I have to tell you something. I'm putting it in a letter, but I want to say it to you, too. If you don't come back with the intention of marrying me, you are going to have to let me go. Just be honest and fair with me, Walter. If you don't want to marry me, it's okay. I understand, no hard feelings. We've had a great ride, but if you don't marry me, you've gotta let me go."

I had a meeting scheduled the next day with Matt Leonetti, the cameraman for Brett Ratner, who did the *Rush Hour* series among other great films—very famous director of photography. That night, I called my lawyer over. Gary says, "What is it, Walt?"

"I'm going home," I told him. "I've gotta let this go. Something else is more important in my life right now."

He says, "What do we tell these people?"

"Tell them something came up."

Gary thought I was nuts, but I took two planes (two planes means up and down and up and down). I hate planes like other people hate planes because you're not in control, but I made it home. Diana's in shock when she sees me. "What's wrong with you? What about the movie?" she asks me.

I told her I didn't want to lose her. "If you want to get married, we'll get married." That was in October, and we were married the week after Thanksgiving on November 27, 1999. It took me fifty-one years to get what I got now.

When I made that step to marry Diana, I knew I was never going to get better on the inside. My friends would tell me I wasn't going to change. I'm trying, though. Like I said, I'm a recovering thief and a long-time wise guy. That's the world I know, but Diana's focus on what's worth something in life keeps me straight.

For example, Diana would tell you that a sit-down is nonsense. "It's big men playing little boys' games," she calls it. When they take it to the test and somebody gets hurt, it's no longer a game, but she calls it playing cops and robbers. She even insulted my friends one time. "It's ridiculous. It's all a bunch of nonsense," is what she said to them.

My friend, Tommy, looks at me, and he says, "You're marrying this girl? She's insulting us."

"Well, she doesn't believe in us, Tommy. She thinks we're idiots. She doesn't like what we do," I explained. "That's why I love her."

I respected Diana's wishes when it came to our wedding. She didn't want my old friends being there, and I didn't blame her for that. That was a time of honesty and legitimacy in our lives, and I honored her feelings. I know where I come from; I'm not denying that. "You're not going to let me bring mud into your house, are you?" I got that line from *Mr. Lucky.*

I'll make my marriage work this time. I want to go out that way. I've cheated on every woman I've ever had. I'm done with all the adultery and cheating nonsense. That won't make up for all the wrongs I've committed. I'm still a Frankenstein sometimes, but I think I've mastered the infidelity. It took three former marriages, numerous girlfriends, and here I am saying this at 59. That's a long time to take to master something.

My wife is probably the only spot in my life that's worth anything. She's not caught up in the garbage. Diana has been through this journey with me for the last fourteen years, and somehow she stays focused on the good. She didn't come with me because I was some infamous jewel thief or would-be millionaire. Diana looked beyond all that. She got inside, you know, where I live. Nobody else ever got there. They didn't earn it like she has.

Sometimes Diana thinks that I married her because of my dad, because she reconnected us. She's always questioned whether I've felt there needed to be some kind of commitment because of that. That's not why I married her, but that action on her part was probably the kindest, most generous thing that anybody ever did for me.

As the story goes, Diana and I were at my house one night and the phone rang. It was in another area of the house, and I heard a familiar voice on the answering machine. My cousin, Billy, was saying that my dad was in the hospital. Though he didn't know exactly what had happened, he thought it was a heart attack.

We knew my dad was in Reno, Nevada, at the time, but we didn't know how to reach him.

The doctors decided it was a bad reaction from mixing his medications, and he was supposed to be getting out of the hospital real soon. My older sister, Linda, had been communicating with Diana, and they spoke about my father. Diana finds out from Linda how to call him directly, and she calls him. Because she was throwing a forty-eighth birthday party for me, this must have been in January, and Diana was asking him to come back for it. She tells him, "This is going to be a surprise. Walter doesn't know that I'm calling you, Mr. Shaw."

"Are you his girlfriend?" he asked her.

"No, I'm just a friend, and I'd love to have you with us. I'll pay for it. If I send you a ticket, will you come here for a visit? You could stay in my townhouse, not with Walter, and you'll have your own room," she told him.

Because he was a little hesitant at first, she told him she'd call him back. Diana had never met him or talked to him before then, but he agreed to make the trip. When Diana found my father, his cancer had come out of remission.

I might never have seen my father again had it not been for my wife, and I will always be grateful to her for that. Just like my father had decades earlier, I'd have gotten the call from my sisters that he had died. Maybe not on the Bowery, but as the story goes, it might have been under a bridge or in a bus station. No doubt, the day I met Diana was the best day of my life.

With Diana at September's in 1993.

Diana's Sons, Adam and Jason, in 1994.

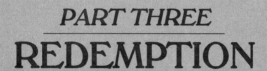

PART THREE
REDEMPTION

PREFACE TO PART THREE

"How do you know they're gonna rob me, Thiel?"
—Walter L. Shaw

So that's how it happened that my dad came back into my life, and I will always remember what he told me when I saw him again for the first time. He says, "I want to tell you something, Thiel."

I ask him, "What's that?"

"I've got about eighteen months to live, and I don't want us to end this way," he tells me. True to his word, after being estranged for twenty-five years I had eighteen months with my father before he died. We had seen each other once in a while, but there's no denying that we were estranged. I was never mad at him for that; I was mad at me. I wanted to axe myself, cut myself up at the end. I chose to lose those years with him. My dad didn't want us to be estranged, but he had no control over what I was doing with my life. The saddest part of our story is our drifting apart. I had a father, but my father had no son. I know that.

Even at the end, though, that poor old man was trying to be an entrepreneur. The Pakistani government was trying to update their archaic phone system, and two British men were involved in that. They owned property in Miami Beach, and some woman put them in touch with my dad. Even knowing how sick he was, they wanted him to design a vital link for them in the construction of earth stations for Pakistan's communications network. I think they had some connection with the government over there.

When my dad was getting involved with them, his attorney, Nathan Barone, calls me and says, "Your dad's negotiating a deal in my office right now, Walt."

I tell him, "I'll be there in half an hour." So I drove down there, and I'll never forget those two British guys. I stormed into Nathan's office and interrupted them saying, "You're looking to go into business with my father?"

"Yes, we are," says one of them. "Your dad's brilliant. He's got some wonderful ideas for our stations, and we're prepared to put up a quarter million dollars for research and development."

I didn't care about any of that. "Let me just tell you something. I am his son, and if you rob this old man, I will kill both of you. I won't have you arrested; I won't take you to jail; I won't sue you; I will shoot both of you in the head in front of God, your wife, your kids and anybody else I can find if you rob this old man." Even then, I'm still passing out threats like a wise guy.

They looked at me, they looked at my dad, and they said, "We have no intention of robbing your father. We're trying to do a legitimate business deal here." I'd heard it all before.

My dad is shaking his head, and I call him out in the hallway. I says to him, "Dad, what is this about?"

And he answers, "You just won't change."

"You won't either," I tell him.

Then he asks, "How do you know they're gonna rob me, Thiel?"

"I don't trust anyone, Dad. I'm not trying to get anything from this. I hope they give you zillions, but I'm not going to let anybody rob you again, not at the end."

Like he tells me on his deathbed, he still had that "Will Rogers mentality." He never met a man he didn't like and all that, but he just seemed to pick a lifetime of people who would rob him of his ideas and run away with the money. My dad's ideas were his, but once he made a prototype, big business thought they had a license to steal. In 2000, a major U.S. corporation stole his last major invention, the prototype for a voice print recognition system, when the patent expired. He applied for that patent in May 1984. Why were people allowed to do what they did to my father?

Hours and hours he'd spend in his spaghetti strap T-shirts. "Now it's ready to be demonstrated," he'd say. They thought they could do whatever they wanted to that poor man. He never had the money to be diligent in his legal work to protect himself, which left him chasing dollars, always chasing dollars that should have been his.

As the story goes, those two Brits turned out to be legitimate guys, and they put up the money. Unfortunately, my dad ends up in a wheelchair a few months later.

CHAPTER THIRTY-TWO

"He found my office, gave me this phony check, and I took it."
—Mike Miller

Back when Diana first picked him up from the airport, she noticed ink stains on my dad's shirt from carrying leaky pens in his pocket. He was always drawing his little sketches with those. The lining was torn in his jacket, and because of the holes, there was paper stuffed in the bottom of his shoes. Even so, he was trying his best to make a good impression. First thing, though, he calls Diana by the name of Barbara, my former wife. It didn't bother her any, but he was humiliated.

When she got him to her house, he kept saying to Diana, "Are you sure this is okay?" Diana's children were quite young then. Jason must have been around three, and Adam was six. Her daughter, Karina, was grown and gone by then. She got my dad settled, and a nanny was coming in the daytime to watch the kids while Diana was at work.

I arrived home from a quick trip to Vegas the day after she picked him up, and that night we all got together for dinner. It was just a few days after that when Diana spoke to my dad about coming back to stay. I had no clue what was going on in Reno. We never understood why he was staying out there, except that my sister, Crystal, and her two kids were out there with him. Crystal had left Russell, the carpet installer, for Dale, the drug addict. She was doing drugs with him, thinking that he'd quit for her if she did them and quit for him.

When Diana asked my father to come back and stay with us for a while, she says, "I'm not asking you for anything. You can just live in my townhouse and be near Walter this way. I'm already paying the mortgage and the utilities, and you have your Social Security checks to do whatever you want to do on your own."

He says to her, "Let me think about it."

We didn't know that he was trying to figure out what to do about Crystal. Crystal and her kids had been a focal point for my mother, who must have told him to look after them when she was gone. That had to be it given what we would later learn about his life out there. But my dad decided to come back to Florida, and he later invited them to follow him to Fort Lauderdale. Without any-place to go, Crystal, Dale and the two kids moved in to Diana's, too.

During that period, my father was picking Crystal up at mid-night from one Denny's and then they picked Dale up at another Denny's. He was a short-order cook and she was a waitress. As sick as he was, my dad was doing that for them. In fact, the first time I ever saw my father get flustered was a night he was going to be late picking them up. Seeing what that was doing to him, I said, "They gotta leave, Dad. They gotta find a motel or go back to Reno. You're too sick to be doing this."

I told Crystal, "You can't live here. You need to find a motel. Dad can't take this."

So Crystal and Dale went back to Reno, and my dad starts slipping. She kept calling collect for his Social Security checks, though, and he kept sending them to her. Finally, six or seven weeks before he died, he tells me, "Thiel, you gotta take the phone calls. I can't take them anymore." My dad never knew how to say no to the apple of his eye. I remember telling Crystal not to call again, and Diana put a block on her calls.

During that period when my dad was back in my life, he actually went to an acquaintance of mine to borrow $3,000. The guy tells me, "I loaned three grand to your dad, Walt."

"You did what?" I said.

So I went to my dad, and it was the only time in that period that I got mad and regretted it. I told him, "If you ever borrow any money from my friends again, I will put you on the next plane out of my life."

He had a hurt look on his face, and he says, "Thiel, it's not for me."

"I know who it's for, Dad. You think you're helping her?"

"She was going to be on the street, and she's my daughter, good, bad, or indifferent."

He knew he couldn't have come to me for the money. Not for Crystal he couldn't, no doubt about it. So I said, "Okay, forget about it. I'll pay the guy." And I did.

My father wrote a bad check for $1,000 to another partner of mine, Mike Miller, a dear friend. Mike kept it in a drawer, and he gave it to me as a goof after my dad died. He calls me into his office and says, "Here," and throws me a bad check.

"He came down to your office and asked you for money?" I couldn't believe it.

"Yeah, he found my office, gave me this phony check, and I took it," Mike tells me.

"You never even cashed it?" I asked him.

"No. I knew there was no money there."

I said, "You knew that when you took it?"

"Yeah, I knew it. Look, it was your father, Walter. I knew how much you loved him."

My dad had tunnel vision when it came to Crystal and her son and daughter. Diana's boys had spent some time around those kids when they were staying with them in Fort Lauderdale, and they had sensed that something strange was going on in their lives, something different. We didn't find out what that was for a number of years.

For one thing, my dad, Crystal and her kids lived under a bridge in Reno for a while. They would jump from motel to motel on his Social Security check, and they'd soak that until they were thrown out. Crystal had a real routine going, but he never discussed that with me, never.

Right before he died, my father wanted to see Crystal one more time. He was in a wheelchair, and he says, "Thiel, I need a favor."

"Dad, please," I says to him, knowing where it was going.

"Crystal got arrested, and she's in jail. I want you to get her out for me," he said.

"You gotta be kidding me, Dad. Please don't ask me to do this."

"No, I want to see her," he told me. "Please, Thiel, for me."

Only because he asked for it did Crystal get to see my father. She was in jail for drugs, and I called her probation officer. When you get out on bond, you can't leave the city, but I said to him, "My dad is dying, and I need my sister here."

He says, "Okay, I'm going to trust you that you'll sign for her and you'll make sure she surrenders and comes back here." I told him I would do that, used my house for security to bond her out, and I brought her back to Florida. I wouldn't let her husband come, but she and the kids moved into the house with us again.

So I made sure Crystal was there when my dad was dying, but she left after that. I haven't seen her since. I'm not trying to hurt anybody here. But like I said, life doesn't keep secrets. It is what it is, and that part of Crystal's life deeply affected my dad's. I hear she got cleaned up back in Reno, which she should be proud of, and she has a full-time job now. Dale is cleaned up, too, and he's working. Linda helped raise Crystal's son, and the daughter went to live with her father, Crystal's first husband, Russell.

Crystal's son later told us that they'd been living in bus terminals before we contacted my father. "You know," he tells us, "you can stay at Trailways during certain hours, and you can go to Greyhound, too. You can skip around and live in those. That's where we were staying some of the time."

"You were doing what?" I asked him. This was three years after my father died, and when I heard that it was like somebody stabbed me. That is the way he was living at the end of his life. No wonder he took Diana up on coming home to us. He was seventy-six or so years old, and he'd have a roof over his head. This is a man who contributed so much to our telecommunications industry, and he was bunking in bus stations and sleeping under bridges at the end. That is how society let him go.

My nephew says to me, "Grandpa never wanted you to know."

CHAPTER THIRTY-THREE

"I'll kiss your mother and tell her you're coming."
—Walter L. Shaw

When it came to my father dying, I asked for one more day, but I didn't get it. In my earlier tough guy talk, I remember saying to the doctor, "If he dies, you're going with him." I knew his doctor couldn't save him, though; my dad had terminal cancer. While watching his favorite minister on television, Walter L. Shaw—genius inventor, complete unknown—passed away on Sunday morning, July 21, 1996.

I'll never get over what he did for me at the end. We were all gathered around his bed together: the pastor, Diana, my sisters. We were all there, and he managed to raise himself up. He couldn't speak anymore, but with his arms flailing, he threw them around me and hugged me. It was like he was saying, "I forgive you, Thiel. Let me go now. It's all right. I'm ready."

My father wanted to be with my mother. He was very clear about that. Him hugging me like that, though, was like his final gift to me. I didn't have to live the rest of my life wondering if he forgave me. He was calling me back with his gesture at the end. You know, a father to a son. After all the things I'd done to hurt him, he was bringing me back to him. What more do you need to know about a guy?

God said *no* to one more day with my dad. That was God's timing, and that was going to be the day. The world hasn't looked the same to me since. The stars grew dimmer when he died.

Delivering his eulogy was the most difficult thing I've ever done. I spoke from my heart and from scripture, and I remember saying, "They don't make guys like him anymore." Crystal sang "Amazing Grace," and Pastor Cohron spoke, too. We also played

"In the Living Years." You know, "Tell them in the living years how much you love them." One of his favorite songs was Perry Como singing "Wind Beneath My Wings," and we played that, too. Those songs meant something to my father.

If you'll remember, those two British guys had put up the R&D money for the Pakistani phone project, and then my dad dies. Unbelievably, in their Rolls Royce and their Bentley, they show up at his funeral. I walked back after the service, and I said, "I can't believe you guys are here. Is this about the money?"

One of them said, "Walter, we came because we knew what your father was. We don't care about the money. Money comes and goes. We lost a quarter million, whatever we put up in the research and development, and your dad died in the middle of it. We did what we did for the pleasure of being in business with him. He was brilliant." They washed the money and took it as an honor to know him as long as they did.

There is no telling what my dad might have done for Southern Bell had they treated him right. You know, with all the money they had for research and development, but I guess they got it all anyway.

Before he died, I had said, "Dad, we never talked about where you want to be buried."

"There's only one place I want to be."

"Where's that?" I asked him.

"I don't have to tell you," he answered.

So I went down to my mother's crypt at Southern Memorial Park in North Miami. It had been ten years. There was a body next to hers, and I told the guy nicely, "You can move it, or I'll move it, but my father has to go there. If I move it, you won't find it; if you move it, you'll know where it's at." Admitting that is embarrassing to me now, but the guy moved it for me.

Like I told you, my mother used to address all her letters to my dad, "Your darling wife to her inventive husband." On my dad's plaque it says, "Your Inventive Husband." They are there together, and I know they're in heaven together, too.

When my dad lost his voice at the very end, he would blink to let me know he knew I was there. But the week before he died he was still able to whisper, and he said softly, "I'll kiss your mother and tell her you're coming, Thiel."

I said to him, "You think you'll see her, Dad?"

"I know I will. She's waiting for me." My dad was a believer to the end.

One day after my father died, Dr. Katzell told me, "You know, your dad was on the morphine patch to help with his pain."

"I know that," I told him.

"Because he wanted to be able to talk to you, though, he wouldn't let me increase the dose. Had I increased it, he would have been sleeping most of the time. His pain threshold was remarkable." So even when he was dying in severe pain, he did that quietly, a gentleman to the end.

My dad knew I was trying to do a movie about him and me, and this is what I've been getting to. Years earlier, you'll remember I'd been approached by Eddie Egan to do a film about my life. It wasn't until Mickey Rourke came into it that I began to take the idea seriously. I met Mickey in 1990. He was still full of life then, and he wanted to play me in a movie. Mickey said, "You've got a fantastic story, Walter. How do you see it playing out?"

I told him I thought it was a good story, too, but my dad had to be a big part of it. Mickey knew what I wanted to do, and I think he should get some credit for it, but he still wanted to make it about heisting. I'm saying it again, though: It's more than that; it's the story of a father and a son.

I was actually in L.A. working on the movie project when I
got the call that my dad was really failing in 1996. Just about to
give up the Hollywood dream anyway, I cancelled everything I had
in the works at the time. I remember saying, "Look, my dad's
dying, and I'm going home." I took the next flight out when they
told me he couldn't walk anymore. That was in April or May, and
he died in July. My need to tell our story was even more profound
after my father died.

The last photo taken of my father and me, May 1996.

CHAPTER THIRTY-FOUR

"We'll always have Paris."
—Humphrey Bogart in *Casablanca*

There was an article in the *Miami Herald* not long ago, in which it was stated: "The only things the Dinner Set Gang has left are big ideas for movies and supposed books in the works." I didn't like the way they said that, but there's some truth to it.

I heard that Don was writing a book, and I ran into him one day. I asked, "Who cares about us being jewel thieves? What's the story in that? That's what we were, and there's no story in that. You were a musician, you got caught up, you married one of the twins, and then you became a criminal. Where's the arc?"

"What's that mean, Walt?" he asked me.

"You have to have a beginning, an arc and a happy conclusion in a good story. Where's the arc in being a jewel thief? Everybody's done a movie about a jewel thief."

Goodfellas, Bugsy, Casino—those movies were done after the characters were killed. They were mob stories, and in those movies, the bad guys were all killed. They got their just desserts by being whacked. That's the arc in those stories. That's the happy ending for the public. In my movie, it makes for some exciting action scenes and a chance to get into a criminal's mind, but nobody cares about the jewel thief. I have been on this journey to make a movie about him and me for nineteen years, and the character that people care about is my father.

I went through a lot looking for a screenwriter. Most writers lose sensitivity to this story. Everybody sees a wise guy story, and that's not what this is about. I had these two writers come down to see me one time, and after they heard some of the horror stories, they locked themselves in their room that night. They were so scared they barricaded their door, afraid they were going to write something that would get them killed. The point I'm making here is that they're not getting the story.

I had ten writers before I met Greg Marquette, a screenwriter and producer/director working in Hollywood. After some years working in Canada for Global Television, CBC Television, BBC Television and the Canadian Television Network, he moved to Hollywood and produced, directed and/or wrote for production companies, producers and major motion picture studios. In fact, he directed *Innocents* for Cinerenta and First Look Pictures, and recently completed the motion picture screenplay for the life story of Tennessee Williams, soon to be a major motion picture. But Greg was the first one who got the arc in this story about my dad and me. He felt the pulse, the relationship in it. It's not about the mob. This is a human interest story. Every father and son in America can identify with us. If you're a father or a son, in a good relationship or bad, an underworld character or a banker on Wall Street, you can relate to this story. Same goes for every wife and mother. This ain't just another *Bronx Tale*.

We have $6,000,000 for the movie, and I need another $4,000,000. I am the holdup. They want to get rid of me. Once again, it's all about my past—who I am and all that. They don't want my dad in the Inventors Hall of Fame because of who he was, and they don't want me around the movie because of who I am.

The past. It's always beating us to death. They gotta bang me with the burglarizing, and my father will forever be remembered for the black box. My dad doesn't deserve to bear that cross. Because he was so screwed the world should forgive my father for his involvement in organized crime. I should be bearing the cross, I know. There is no doubt about it. Every time it comes up, though, it's like being re-sentenced to a life in prison. But I guess

I should be hearing some of what I said to that kid in my prison cell. You know, what did I expect from being a criminal?

People want to look at the wise guys, test us and poke at us, but they're not going to have us come home, you know. It's that simple. They are fascinated with the world we're in, but we're never going home with them. Why would you want to bring mud into your house?

The tagline for *Catch Me if You Can* calls it "the true story of a real fake." Steven Spielberg directed it, supposedly inspired by the life story of Frank Abagnale, the con artist. They weren't even going to let Abagnale into the Oscars. If I ever made it with my movie, I would probably have to fight to get passes to the Oscars, too. They don't deal with the talent; they buy them off. Abagnale was given $750,000 or $800,000 for the story, and that movie made $140,000,000.

Another option I've been given is to sell the script. One of the best producers in Hollywood has offered me $1,500,000 for my script. Another icon offered me a million, and he's been nominated for Oscars in writing, directing and producing. Years ago, a representative of Paramount Pictures offered me $850,000 for my screenplay. I remember saying to her, "They accused us of stealing $70,000,000 in jewels. Do you think I'm impressed by $850,000 for a screenplay?"

I've seen real money in my life, and I'm only asking $300,000 to produce it. That's it! It's not like I'm holding them up for some big ransom here. I get twenty points of the backend after producer's fees are paid. In other words, say the movie costs $10,000,000 to make; we have to net $20,000,000 for the investor to get his money back. After all debt is paid, then I share 20 percent of what's left over. I'll never see big money again. I know that. But this time, it's not about the money. It's about my father's legacy. I want his name in the history books.

I'm not going to sell the movie. I won't let Hollywood just do whatever they want with it. Because I'm not going to let them tarnish my dad's voice, I won't get out of the way. I don't care what they do with me, but they're not going to put four-letter words in his mouth. He didn't talk that way, but Hollywood wants him to talk that way.

My dad was a gentleman all the time. He was never foul-mouthed and wouldn't say a bad word about anybody. The hardest word I ever heard him call somebody was "scumbag." He never said bad words. I remember him looking at me and saying, "Why do you say that?" When I would go off on my tirades, he would tell me, "Think it out before you say it, Thiel. You can't take the words back."

He wouldn't have cigarettes and cigars in his mouth, either, and I know that would happen on the big screen. They are not going to defame him in any kind of way, and if this dream ever comes true, I'm going to be there to make sure of that. If it gets made, I'm calling the movie *A License to Steal*—same as the book—and it's as close to being made as it's ever been. Nevertheless, it still remains a dream until it happens. It may never happen, or I may be long gone when it does. A book will stand, though. Barbra Streisand said something I love: "You want to do things in life that stand the test of time." Her movie, *The Way We Were*, stands the test of time. You can watch that movie and forget about when it was made.

Back when I was negotiating with Paramount in 1996, I was told, "Get the book written, and I guarantee this movie will happen." I should have started with a book twenty years ago, but I didn't think I could do it. In finally getting this done, at least my father will rest in history permanently. Long after we're gone, our kids and grandchildren will read this. They don't have to like Walter Shaw Jr. There's nothing admirable about me. I have been a real Frankenstein, and I just woke up in the last act of my life.

But his descendants will love and respect my father for what he was trying to do with his life.

I should say here that, in addition to all the monsters, I've also been around a lot of good guys in my time. The guys who have backed me in my dreams for a movie are legitimate. They've taken a gamble on me because they believe in the project. They're only writing checks because they appreciate the story. If I'm in there as a producer and they get a few dollars out of it, they'll do it. They've never done it for selfish reasons; they recognize that my dad was a genius out of step with his times.

Mike Miller, Meyer Lansky, and Jack Cooper founded the Hollywood Seminole Bingo Hall. Mike was the creator and designer, and he treated me like I was his son. He backed my dream about the movie, and he financed my livelihood and development costs for eight years. Mike dying soon after my father died was probably the third hardest blow in my life. We met on a handshake, and he financed *It Takes a Thief to Stop a Thief*. He gave me $85,000 in cash to make that video.

"We haven't got a contract," I said to him.

"I don't need a contract; I know who you are and where you come from. Go make your dream," he tells me. When I went to him for the money to pay a retainer fee to Mickey Rourke to act in the movie, Mike came up with it. Mike was there every step of the way for me.

Because he saw how badly I took my dad's death, Mike waited until the end of his own life to tell me he had cancer, too. Finally he called me over one day. Holding a piece of paper, he says, "Walt, I've got a significant investment in the movie, and it's all yours. All debts are forgiven." He died a few days later.

Because he believes in the project, Frank Vincent of *The Sopranos* has been with me since 1999, and he was kind enough to write the foreword for this book. The generosity of others has always been about my dad, though. I've been blessed that way, and he's been gone since 1996.

A good example of the injustice done concerning my dad's inventions is something that happened to me at the Pompano Race Track. After 9/11, a guy came to see me at my office there. He happens to own a very large video conferencing company. He walks in, and I'm thinking he's going to offer to help finance the movie. That's why I took the meeting. Instead, he says, "I wanted to thank you personally, Walter. Your father created the conference call. I use it in my video conferencing, and I am doing great numbers since 9/11. People don't want to get on planes anymore."

"What does that mean exactly?" I asked him.

"Well, I just wanted to thank you and your father," he told me.

I said, "How about penning me a check to finish the movie about him?"

"I don't invest in movies," he answered.

And I asked, "How much did you do last year?"

"About 150 million," he tells me.

The invention that would have changed my family's life forever was the conference call. That was the big one for my father, and all I needed was another $4,000,000 to tell his story.

When Greg Marquette finished writing a dynamite first draft script, I sent it out. I had borrowed the money from a wonderful doctor, one of the kindest men I've ever known. He met me on a Monday and paid Greg on Wednesday, also without a contract. Actors such as William Hurt, Sir Ben Kingsley, and Stephen Dorff all expressed interest in becoming attached, saying it was one of the best scripts they'd ever read. We packaged the film and a rep from a major Canadian production company contacts me and tells me they want to do the film.

"Great," I tell them. So they come down, sending their executive producer over to meet me at the racetrack. They verbally commit before they write up an agreement, but then they said, "There's a catch."

"Yeah, what's that?"

"We want to take the film to Canada and shoot it," he told me.

I learned something from that. If you take a film into Canada, they'll give you half your budget. You never have to pay it back if you shoot your movie there and use the required staff from Canada. But there is no way I'm taking my movie to Canada. My dad was a true American patriot, a colonel. It's an American story. We were born here. We both got a blessing that way. So I wasn't doing that. If my dad was alive, he wouldn't want me to do that. I won't take my film to Canada.

I knew I could lose my film by doing that. Of course, we had all the paperwork completed, the shooting was to begin in January 2001, and I had to call the powers that be to tell them I would not go to Canada. There were a bunch of articles written about it in Florida. Even the film commission in Palm Beach says to me, "Is this really what you want to do?"

"I'm not going to Canada," I told them.

It's principle above all other things. It's not about the money with me on this movie. You can't buy my integrity, and I won't tamper with my dad's.

A lot of guys would have grabbed that golden opportunity and said, "Hey, I'll go to Canada. Forget integrity, forget America." But on my film, it's going to say "Made in America." You know, that's just the way it is, and it's cost me five or six more years of my life by my being principled.

I got that all the way back when I was with the wise guys. Anthony says, "Don't judge me by what's in my pocket or what title I hold; be a friend, good or bad, and I'll make you, right or wrong, if you're my friend." Sometimes I'm too stubborn because of that, but I still go by those principles.

I have never felt as much rejection and pressure as I have felt trying to get this project going. Even more than the tension of pulling off any burglary in my lifetime, this has caused me the greatest stress. There can't be too many things more difficult than dealing with the movie industry, but I'm still working on it. Unlike me, I'm hopeful it will get made some day. I've made it past forty, and this is my only goal at this point.

Telling this here might be giving something away, but I want the movie to end at the old Riverside Hotel on Las Olas Boulevard in Fort Lauderdale. Years ago, I read that the guy who made the TV tube received a proclamation posthumously. I didn't know what that meant, but the lady who did it for that guy was from New Jersey, and I called her. She says, "Walter, we finally got him recognized for his achievements, but it was quite a process. You have to gather a lot of recommendations and other things. It can be done, but it takes years."

I figured there was another way to skin the cat, so I called Senator Dan Jenkins, the retired Florida state senator who introduced me to E.J. Daniels, and he was willing to talk to me. With his help, my dad was honored with a proclamation on what would have been his eighty-third birthday, December 20, 2000.

That summer, I called Frank Vincent, and I told him I wanted to throw a banquet to recognize the proclamation my dad had received. I wanted to know if he and some of the other guys from *The Sopranos* like Chuck Zito, Vinny Vella, Nick Puccio and Mickey Bruno could make it. He says, "We'll be delighted."

I had just done *The Montel Williams Show* about two months prior, and I invited him, too. Montel saw me on *Oprah*, and he asked me to do his show the same way. I think he was attracted to the down-and-out story, and we became friends after that. That's why he and his executive producer came down to give us their endorsement that day.

SENATOR DAN JENKINS

TO ALL THIS MAY CONCERN:

Walter Lewis Shaw, a man who has been sadly overlooked, but were it not for his character the whole world would have stood up and acknowledged him long before now. A man of quiet stature, his humble nature was foremost in the way he handled himself and his inventions thus preventing him the monetary rewards and notoriety he deserved before his death. Walter looked far beyond the present time and had the ability 20 to 30 years ago to create some of the most frequently used telephonic features of this day; the conference call, the speaker phone and call forwarding, just to name a few.

Walter Shaw followed in the brilliance of men like Alexander Graham Bell in setting the pulse for the communication industry. His genius was recognized in many circles; this being evidenced by President Eisenhower in 1954 when Walter was hired to create the emergency alert system; the red-phone as it is better known, which is still used today by the White House. His employment within the military ranks was too short to afford him a Pension and his business ways were too trusting and short-sighted to allow him to protect the inventions he created from being exploited by the fast-paced business people he came into contact with.

Mr. Shaw was acknowledged with a Degree as Doctor of Humanities granted by the Trustees of Coral Ridge Baptist University on January 6, 1996 - too late in his life for him to fully appreciate the accreditation this bestowed upon him; Walter lost his battle to Prostate Cancer in July of that same year.

Mr. Shaw was also given a Tribute by Florida House of Representative Stephen R. Wise, who acknowledged him as *"a man out of step with the times in which he lived"*.

It is important that we recognize Walter Lewis Shaw posthumously. We should also know that each time you reach for the telephone or many of the features available, Mr. Shaw made it possible for us to have these now - rather than later. He has provided us with a foundation in the telecommunications industry which reaches into our universe and shall never be forgotten.

Sincerely,

SENATOR DAN JENKINS

Senator Daniel Leslie Jenkins passed away on November 18, 2007. Dan never judged me, and even when I fell down he stuck by me. He also did more than anyone to help my father receive the recognition he deserved. I will always be grateful to Dan, and regret that he did not get the chance to realize the publication of this book.

Florida House of Representatives

Tribute

A Tribute to Walter L. Shaw, Sr.

WHEREAS, Walter Shaw has been described as "a man out of step with the times in which he lived," as he was far ahead of the rest of the scientific community in the world of electronics, conceptualizing 25 years ago voice and data transmission technologies regarded as commonplace today; and

WHEREAS, not only was Walter Shaw unique in his talent, skills, and knowledge, but in his personality, as well, seeing only the best in everyone and always willing to give unselfishly of himself; and

WHEREAS, though there were some who would exploit his kindness, many who knew him remember that, regardless of whatever life dealt him, Walter Shaw was a man who always wore a warm smile and offered a cordial handshake; and

WHEREAS, born on December 20, 1917, Walter Shaw is noted for his accomplishments in the communications industry through his work as a radio station manager and disc jockey at WKWF Radio, as a senior systems supervisor and field project engineer at Datapoint, and as a senior systems installation engineer with the military at Andrews Air Force Base, just to name a few; and

WHEREAS, Walter Shaw has been granted 39 patents for various types of telephone, communications, and dialing apparatuses, including conference call equipment, call forwarding, speaker phone, and a two-way communication unit, and patents are pending on a remote dialing apparatus and a voice print recognition system; and

WHEREAS, it is fitting and proper that honor be accorded a man who has had such an impact both in his field and on the people with whom he has come in contact during his lifetime. NOW, THEREFORE,

BE IT RESPECTFULLY PROCLAIMED that sincerest appreciation and gratitude be expressed for the accomplishments of Walter Shaw, a kind and giving man, who helped open the door to the electronic age.

Stephen R. Wise
Representative, District 13

I wanted to do something special on that occasion, and a friend gave me the name of a sculptor who could make a bust of my dad. So I go to this artist, Yaacov Heller, and I tell him what I want to do. "Okay," he tells me, "it costs $150,000, but I'll do it for $100,000." It was just a normal job to him, but he cut the price for some reason. Turns out Yaacov Heller is one of the most famous sculptors in the world. He has sculpted a lot of famous people.

Yaacov did some research and found out more about my dad. One day he said, "Your dad was quite a guy, Walt. No wonder you're doing this for him." He started making the mold, and it came to life, bringing out my dad's spirit in the wax.

The first time I saw it, I broke down crying. "You captured my father," I told him.

When it came time to pay him, Mr. Heller says to me, "Just pay me for my costs and we'll call it a day." That included the cast and everything else. In other words, "I believe in your father's story. You owe me nothing."

The banquet took place at the Riverside Hotel on June 27, 2003. I rented a room, and three hundred people attended. Some of the wise guys came. As Frank Vincent promised, he and some of the cast from *The Sopranos* showed up. Senator Stephen R. Wise, a member of Florida's House of Representatives, and his mother were there, and the Palm Beach and Broward County film commissioners showed up, too. We unveiled the bust of my father that day. All kinds of newspapers, news shows, and magazines covered the story. It was a great way of acknowledging what my dad had given to a society that took everything from him.

I'm trying to get something across here. I don't look at society the way most people do. Most people think our society is honest, law abiding and righteous—you know, made up of rights and wrongs. I don't see it that way. I don't think society gave my dad a fair break. You can see me as a Frankenstein, but I see myself as a

product of what society made me. If my dad got what he had coming, I wouldn't be writing this. He was entitled to it. He worked for
it. And I don't separate recognition for what he invented from the
money that should have come his way. He should have got it all.

It was about time for him to get recognized like that. Now it's
time to tell the whole story of a man who got nothing for all the
times he said, "Now it's ready to be demonstrated." I might never
get a movie made, and my father's story might have been lost if I'd
never gotten this book written. But it's written, and like
Humphrey Bogart said to Ingrid Bergman in *Casablanca*, "We'll
always have Paris."

In Honor and Loving Memory of
WALTER LEWIS SHAW, SR
☎ *Because of Whom the Bells Toll Afar* ☎
A Genuine Telecommunications Engineering Genius —
Inventor-of-Record for 39 US Patents, including
many key elements of modern telephone systems.
Inventor ★ Father ★ Son's Hero
December 20, 1917—July 21, 1996

World-renowned sculptor, Yaacov Heller.

Taking my turn at the podium,
Riverside Hotel, Fort Lauderdale, Florida.

Standing between Yaacov's sculpture and one of my dad's framed
patents—one of the proudest moments of my life.

Paying tribute to Yaacov.
Left to right: Walter, Yaacov Heller, Montel Williams, Chuck Zito, Vinny Vella, Frank Vincent, Nicholas Puccio and Tom Madden.

Left to right: Vinny Vella, Joe Maruzzo, Chuck Zito, Montel Williams, Frank Vincent and Nicholas Puccio.

*Some heartfelt words
from Montel Williams.*

*Gregory Marquette,
Screenwriter,* A License to Steal.

Left to right: Teddy Powder, Bert Schneiderman and Tom Sobeck.

Linda joined me to remember our dad.

Adam

Jason

Diana

"I might never have seen my father again had it not been for my wife. That action on her part was probably the kindest, most generous thing that anybody ever did for me. No doubt, the day I met Diana was the best day of my life."

The Statement

Walter Lewis Shaw and his patented inventions have allowed the telecommunications industry in the United States to reach unpredictable epic proportions, providing the public with unprecedented telephonic features well in advance of the technology at that time. Devices, commonly referred to as the Automatic Hands-Free Speaker Phone a/k/a Two-Way Communication Unit [originally designed for the handicap and donated by Mr. Shaw to the Iron Lung Society], the Telephone Switchboard Call Transfer Device, Conference Call Equipment and Voice Print Recognition System, the later of which was designed by Mr. Shaw in the early 1980s, and has still not reached its unlimited usage. These inventions, to name only a few, have allowed for the advancement of the telecommunication devices and equipment that are widely used today. Mr. Shaw and his inventions have provided a foundation and framework for the telecommunication industry as a whole – an industry that has provided technology used by individuals as well as the corporate giants throughout the United States and the World. Without Mr. Shaw and his contributions to the telecommunications industry, along with the foundation of technology he afforded all of us in providing the various communication devices throughout the world, suffice it to say, the world would not be the same or where it is today.

With the help of Mr. Shaw and his patented inventions, such as Call-Transfer ["Call Forwarding" as it is more commonly known today]; individuals and professionals throughout the world can now communicate with each other, even when they have relocated physically. The same holds true for Conference-Calling, which enables individuals to communicate with several parties simultaneously, eliminating the need for each participant in the conference to be present in the same location. Using Mr. Shaw's conference calling equipment, as well as other telecommunication devices and patents has allowed corporate business to increase their production while minimizing costs – an essential element to the success of any business.

Sadly, the barrier built by Mr. Shaw's humble nature prohibited him and his inventions from receiving, during his lifetime, the recognition that he was so deserving of. That time has now come, with the help of his immediate family, specifically his son, Walter T. Shaw, so that the many inventions which have propelled us to where we are today can finally be acknowledged. By acknowledging Mr. Shaw's documented patents, the thousands of people who handle each device can now know and acknowledge the person solely responsible for the invention and design. In addition, they will be able to acknowledge the sense of security this country had the pleasure of realizing during the Eisenhower Administration with the design and implementation of the "Red Phone" being put in place by Mr. Shaw at the request of the United States Government.

Never before was there a man so deserving, yet so deprived of the benefits as a result of his humble nature and kind spirit. In a posthumous effort, a bust was created to honor his memory and the State of Florida paid him public recognition in the form of a Proclamation. It is with great pleasure the son, Walter T. Shaw, joined by his family, wishes to offer this bust for placement in your facility – for all to read and remember.

Patent Attorney David A. Gast's Statement of Appeal for
Walter Lewis Shaw's Induction into the National Inventors Hall of Fame.

EPILOGUE

My whole life I wanted to know what my father thought about me. I know he hated what I was doing with my life, but I always wondered how he felt about us. When he was confined to bed at the end, I would sneak up by his room and stand there looking at him, a distance off on the stairs. One day he motioned for me. All those years, and by that action, he was going to give me what I waited for all my life.

I walked over to his bed, and before he could speak, I said, "Dad, let me tell you something. I was going down this road long before Archie, long before meeting any of them. It had nothing to do with you. I was born going down this road. At the fork, you went right and I went left. I chose my own direction. So if you think you gotta tell me whatever you think you gotta tell me, rest assured, I went that way on my own. You had nothing to do with it."

I knew he was about to apologize for ever letting me meet those people. My mother always told him that my meeting those "vile" people was the turning point for me. Uncle Archie, in particular, was blamed. But I didn't want my father taking into eternity even the remotest feeling that I went the way I did because of him. I had this gun in my hand way before meeting anybody. He smiled at me and says, "All right, if that's how you feel, Thiel."

I said, "That's how I feel, Dad." Maybe that was my only real gift to him, telling him that he never pulled the trigger for me, that I did that myself.

I went on to say, "We never talked about this, but I have to ask you. Why do you think you never made it like other people who invent great things? I mean, you're right there with Edison."

He says, "Thank you, Thiel." He always said thank you like I just gave him the Nobel Peace Prize or something. He was very humble, my dad, and he goes on saying, "I'd be inhuman if I didn't ponder that. But you know what? I never questioned it. There is a scripture in the Bible, Isaiah 45:9, it says something like: 'Does the clay talk back to the potter?' How does the clay question its maker, Thiel? So I never made it with any of my inventions. I might ask Him why not when I get there, but I just never questioned Him. We don't know why I never reached the pot at the end of the rainbow, but I always felt that God had a purpose for my life."

My dad never expressed anger about any of it. He refused to give in to all the injustices. When he lost his appeals, or when they put an injunction on him, he just went right back to the laboratory and kept working. That was his way of dealing with it: *I'll make something else.*

I've had professionals tell me, "You're imbalanced because you're willing to sacrifice your whole life to get even if somebody hurts your loved ones."

I always answered them, "I'm not willing to wait for what society calls justice."

My father and I had totally opposing viewpoints in terms of revenge or avenging anything. I wanted vengeance, and to the end he tells me to let it go. "Thiel, in the grand scheme of things, it doesn't matter anymore," he says. "I hope you let all this go." He could never think of hurting somebody to get even. I was mad at the world and doing something about it. Like Oprah said to me on her show, "So you were just mad and you started robbing people?"

But my father wasn't mad. He didn't go out kicking and screaming. My dad never had any ill will toward men. People were basically good in his view. Just like Will Rogers, he never met a man he didn't like.

Putting the money issue aside, though, I went on to ask him,

"But why doesn't it matter to you that you didn't get recognition and gratitude for what you did?"

He says, "Thiel, I'm gonna die, but my inventions will live on. They won't die. The speakerphone will live on, the conference call will live on, and call forwarding will live on. A piece of me will always be around. That's all I need to know." My dad never looked for applause. He didn't need to tell his story.

"Are you ever gonna try and do anything with any of my other inventions?" he asks me.

"No," I answered him. "I'm burying them with you. All they ever brought us was heartache and pain. They never gave us anything but that." My father was looking for honesty from me, but I know that wasn't true for him. Every time he solved a problem with one of his inventions, each time he found the missing piece, he found joy in telling us, "Now it's ready to be demonstrated!"

Pastor Cohron preached at my dad's funeral. Fifteen years earlier, I had given a bag to the pastor to keep in a safety deposit box for me. When he came for the service he said, "You probably forgot that you gave this to me, Walt." Still ready to be demonstrated, there it was—the black box.

Forty-six years ago, I sat in that courtroom in the Old Senate Office Building in Washington, D. C., watching my dad getting grilled by Senator McClellan. I was so impressed by the wise guys, wearing their fancy colognes, and my dad's up there in his favorite aftershave, Old Spice. All I've got left of his is a black box and a bottle of Old Spice, but I wouldn't trade either of them for all the jewelry in the world.

I said at the beginning of this book that I always felt like my dad's opposite. He was all the things I was never going to be. My father was a good guy, and I was a wise guy. Telling our story is my shot at redemption.

*"What lies behind us
and what lies before us
are tiny matters
compared to what lies within us."*

—Ralph Waldo Emerson

Acknowledgments

While this story has yet to make it to the silver screen, I would like to thank some very special people who, through the years, have supported the idea through their kindness and generosity.

Gregory Marquette
Frank Vincent
Chuck Zito
Christian Hoff
Mario Van Peebles
James Caan
Edward Lynch
Louis Vanaria
Frankie Valli
Vinny Vella
Vinnie Pastore
Debbie Mazar
Steven Bauer

Additional Thanks

Tony Adler
Attorney Gary Adwar
Ed Arenas
Bill Badalato

Jim Beeson
A true believer, who not only talks the talk but walks the walk.

Selma Blair
Peter Bogdanovich
Justin Bordeaux, AF STUDIOS, LLC

Andrew Borden

Kerry Brewer, Web Stream
For creating my dad's website.

Mickey Bruno

Gary Busey

Daniel J. Coe

Attorney John P. Contini

Matt Dillon

Stephen Dorff

Jack Douglas

Chuck Elderd

Robert Evans

Jeff Goldblum

Robert Greenhut

Bob Gunton

Tobie Haggerty

Richard Halsey

Robin Hommel

William Hurt

Gary James

Senator Dan Jenkins

Val Kilmer

Sir Ben Kingsley

Ted Kurdyla

Martin Landau

Attorney James E. Lewis

Ronnie Lorenzo

Michael Madsen

Myke Michaels

Charles Nicosia

Michael J. Peter

Nicholas Puccio

Ryan Rayston

Anthony B. Richmond

Dan Riemer

Eric Roberts

Mickey Rourke

Keith W. Rouse

Justin Scoppa Jr.

Ray Sharp

Jim Small

Tucker Tooley

Diana Venora

Marco Vitali

Mark Wahlberg

Matthew Weiner

Elizabeth Wentworth

Allan J. & Diane Wertheim

Peter Williams
For being there when you were needed most.

Senator Stephen R. Wise

Special Appreciation

Joe Florea

A true friend and believer. It would be a sin to overlook the kindness you have extended to me over the years. Without hesitation, you have helped me through some of the rough patches, believing in my endeavors, and wanting only the best for my family and me. Joe, my friend, thank you.

Yaacov Heller

Thank you for your dedication, talent and artistry in bringing my father to life in the statue you created for all to admire.

Harold Jones

I wouldn't have made it to this point without your help.

Frank Vincent

You've been my champion. Thank you, my friend.

Montel Williams

A truly unique man, Montel came to stand by me when we celebrated my father's posthumous proclamation and the unveiling of the bust sculpted by Yaacov Heller. I met him for the first time as a guest on *The Montel Williams Show*. He has displayed his strength of character in support of my endeavors, flying to our celebration on his own dime. Believing in my dreams, Montel Williams has never asked for anything in return. My sincerest appreciation, Montel.

Oprah Winfrey

I had the great privilege of being invited to appear on *Oprah* in 2003. It was an honor to share the stage with a true pillar of strength for so many. Oprah continually fights to ensure that the truth is being uttered on her stage. It was especially uplifting to be asked to remain for *Oprah After the Show*, when she was supportive even when the negative was broached by her audience. You are a true lady, Oprah, in all aspects of the definition.

In Memory

Eddie Egan, the real *French Connection* cop

My friend, Eddie, knew a good story when he heard one. He believed long ago that my dad's story needed to be seen by the masses to be truly appreciated. Well, Eddie, it's finally in print.

Darrell L. Jones, Unique Producers

A man of integrity and principles. A true filmmaker of our time.

Michael M. Miller

A beloved friend, mentor and definite believer that my dad's story needed to be told.

About the Author

Known for writing compelling narratives based on true life stories, Mary Jane Robinson has composed more than seventy-five personal histories in the past twenty years. Remaining true to the record, she succeeds in preserving the voice and integrity of each individual as the stories of their lives unfold, finding meaning in every chapter. Mary Jane resides with her family in Naples, Florida, where she founded Story Books, a business committed to helping others preserve their life stories.